William James's
Revolution

William James's
Revolution

A New Perspective on
The Varieties of Religious Experience

Ron Miller

EVAN BLAKE PUBLISHERS

William James's Revolution:
A New Perspective on The Varieties of Religious Experience
Copyright © 2011 by Ron Miller

International Standard Book Number: 978-0-9835421-0-0
Library of Congress Control Number: 2011905786

PRINTED IN THE UNITED STATES OF AMERICA

EVAN BLAKE PUBLISHERS
c/o Common Ground
815 Rosemary Terrace
Deerfield, IL 60015
www. ronmillersworld.org

Cover photograph: Henry James, circa 1905.

DEDICATED
WITH GRATITUDE AND AFFECTION TO
MARJORIE LINDSAY REED
LONG-TIME FRIEND AND
CO-WORKER IN THE VINEYARD

TABLE OF CONTENTS

INTRODUCTION

THE REVOLUTION

When it was first published in 1902, *The Varieties of Religious Experience* caused a revolution, a quantum leap, a paradigm shift. For many of its first readers, and for many later readers as well, the experience was much like believing one day that the heavenly bodies circle around the earth and learning the next day that the earth is but one of several planets orbiting around the sun.

The study of religion would never be the same. How ironic that William James, the man who led this revolution, taught physiology, psychology, and philosophy at Harvard...but never religion. And yet, the Gifford Lectures he delivered in Edinburgh, Scotland, in 1901 and 1902, became the book that launched a thousand others, arguably the most important text about religion written in English in the 20th century.

Until that time, the study of religion revolved largely around an examination of creed, code, and cult. What doctrines or dogmas did a particular religion teach? What were its basic tenets? These elements constituted its creed. What moral stance did it embody? What ethical teachings did it embrace? These precepts formed its code. And, finally, what rituals did it enact? The architecture of its sacred space, the chant, the vestments, the defining liturgical ceremonies...all of these factors revealed its cult.

Eschewing all such traditional foci of investigation and study, James asked a new question. What was the experience of the person or persons standing at the origin of this religious movement? What was the experience of Moses, Jesus, Muhammad, and the Buddha that led to Judaism, Christianity, Islam, and Buddhism?

And the same question can be asked of Teresa of Avila and the Carmelites, Ignatius of Loyola and the Jesuits, George Fox and the Quakers, Mary Baker Eddy and the Christian Scientists, Jaladin Rumi and the Whirling Dervishes, the Baal Shem Tov and the East European Hasidim.

James opened the door to the scientific study of religious experience, probing the relationship between religion and psychology. It is obvious no one can have a religious experience without brain activity. The salient question is whether this brain activity is the mediator or creator of the experience. In other words, is the brain, much like a television set, receiving and transmitting a program not originating in itself? If consciousness—as many sacred traditions claim—constitutes the essential nature of reality, than we are recipients, not creators, of that consciousness.

THE BOOK

This classic text by William James should be required reading for anyone wanting to study religion. But years of college teaching have convinced me that this is a daunting read for most undergraduate students, and even for some older adults. One of my students asked me whether I could translate James's book into English. Perhaps it was that question that first led me to write this book.

I began by selecting passages that I thought did the most to communicate James's most important insights. Readers may disagree on some of the texts either included or omitted, but I'm confident that there will be a fairly strong consensus about most of my choices. These selections (direct quotes from James's book) are presented in page-size portions. The titles, however, are my own.

On the facing page of each portion of James's text, the reader finds a commentary intended to elucidate its central idea. This commentary is derived from my own experience of teaching this text to undergrads for some thirty years. I attempt in these commentaries to bring the philosopher's penetrating insights into the world of a contemporary reader.

There are many editions of James's text with no agreement on pagination. Consequently, I identify the text in terms of where it occurs in the orginal lecture series. James himself uses this division in his book. So if the reader knows that a particular quote comes from Lecture Two, then he can readily find it in any of the many editions of "The Varieties of Religious Experience."

I am grateful to Jim Kepler of Adams Press for making the path to publication as painless as possible. His many years of experience are reflected in his sage advice. Lake Forest College, where I have been teaching for thirty-seven years, has always been generous in providing me both with research funds and student research assistants to support my scholarly endeavors. I am grateful to these dedicated and talented student colleagues: Tim Hacker (class of 2009), Austin Stewart (2010), Evan Piermont (2011), and Fiorella Lopez (2011). I am grateful as well to my children, Jim and Carrie, my son-in-law, Matt, and my grandchildren, Evan and Blake Spezzano.

More needs to be said about my son as a co-worker in all my endeavors. In addition to being that miracle that every child is to its parents, Jim plays a constant and indispensable role in my professional life as teacher and scholar. Despite his intensely busy life, he is always only an email or phone call away, ready to help me in any way he can. I often feel like a medieval monk, led out of the scriptorium where he has spent many years copying manuscripts by hand, into a strange place where printed pages are being belched out of a mysterious mechanism that people call "a printing press." Jim has enabled me to function in a world he inhabits as a native, but a world I enter only occasionally and always as a stranger.

My hope is that this book will entice the reader to study the original and unedited text from cover to cover. But even if some readers go no farther than what is found in these pages, I will be happy in the realization that they have encountered James's seminal thoughts on these important matters. They will inevitably have some sense of the magnitude of the revolution he led.

At this point we are ready to let James speak for himself. I can only hope that my commentary will help the reader to gain insight into James's extraordinary book. On this 26th day of August, the 100th anniversary of James's death, I submit this work to my readers with gratitude for the legacy of this great man.

AUGUST 26, 2010

William James's Revolution

LECTURE I
RELIGION AND NEUROLOGY

1:1 STATEMENT OF INTENT

I am neither a theologian, nor a scholar learned in the history of religions, nor an anthropologist. Psychology is the only branch of learning in which I am particularly versed. To the psychologist the religious propensities of man must be at least as interesting as any other of the facts pertaining to his mental constitution. If the inquiry be psychological, not religious institutions, but rather religious feelings and religious impulses must be its subject, and I must confine myself to those more developed subjective phenomena recorded in literature produced by articulate and fully self-conscious men, in works of piety and autobiography.

I:I

The focused scope of James's inquiry contributes to the unique role of this classic text in the vast library of books on religion. James is laying the foundation of an organized study of religion, where religious testimonies constitute the data for his undertaking. By this we mean direct witness to religious experience, whether autobiographical or in the accounts of others. Neither creeds nor theological systems mark the beginning of this inquiry but religious experience itself in all of its varieties. What did Moses experience on the mountaintop before he descended with the Ten Commandments? What did Jesus experience when he was immersed in the waters of the Jordan and felt the divine spirit descend on him? What did Muhammad experience when he felt himself wrapped in the divine presence in the hills outside Mecca? What did Siddhartha Gotama experience under the tree that led to his awakening? Without these experiences would the sacred traditions that sprang up in their wake have ever arisen?

1:2 GENIUSES IN RELIGION

We must make search rather for the original experiences which were the pattern-setters to all this mass of suggested feeling and imitated conduct. These experiences we can only find in individuals for whom religion exists not as a dull habit, but as an acute fever.... But such individuals are "geniuses" in the religious line.

I:2

Many people know religion only at the level of "imitated conduct." James intends to focus on the religious geniuses, the "pattern setters." There are many artists, but few work with the passion of a DaVinci. There are many musicians, but few compose with the fervor of a Mozart. Not every religious testimony will be explored. James must seek out the exemplars, the pioneers, the ones who are designated as outstanding within the traditions they represent.

The literature available to James at the turn of the twentieth century was much more limited than what is at hand today. Most of his evidence comes from Christian sources. Few voices of Jewish mysticism are heard, nor does this work tap the rich archives of Muslim mysticism. James, of course, is not writing the last word on this topic. In many ways, his greatness lies in the fact that he is the first.

1:3 MEDICAL MATERIALISM

Medical materialism seems indeed a good appellation for the too simple-minded system of thought which we are considering. Medical materialism finishes up Saint Paul by calling his vision on the road to Damascus a discharging lesion of the occipital cortex, he being an epileptic. It snuffs out Saint Teresa as an hysteric, Saint Francis of Assisi as an hereditary degenerate. George Fox's discontent with the shams of his age, and his pining for spiritual veracity, it treats as a symptom of a disordered colon.... Scientific theories are organically conditioned just as much as religious emotions are; and if we only knew the facts intimately enough, we should doubtless see "the liver" determining the dicta of the sturdy atheist as decisively as it does those of the Methodist under conviction anxious about his soul.

1:3

What all too often poisons the waters of research in religion is some kind of reductionist framework implying that religious experience cannot possibly be what it claims to be. Reductionism is a "nothing but-ism" that can take many forms. One of these is what James calls "medical materialism," which dismisses St. Paul as an epileptic and St. Teresa as a hysteric. James makes clear throughout his work that much of the so-called scientific study of religion is anything but scientific. Many, although claiming to be scientists, come to religion with a mind already made up. Since they already "know" that religious experience cannot be real, they have merely to pin down what it is instead. Is it a physiological dysfunction? An unenlightened form of scientific explanation? A psychological compensation? There are numerous possibilities, but the one possibility that can never be entertained by reductionists is that a religious experience might actually be what it claims to be.

James exposes the unscientific nature of this allegedly scientific approach by turning it on its head. If a dysfunctional occipital cortex lies at the origin of religious experience, then perhaps a dysfunctional liver can explain atheism. If all religious experience can be dismissed as organic dysfunction, what protects the experiences of the agnostic and atheist from the same diagnosis? With logic and wit, James shows the intrinsic weakness of this line of thinking so readily embraced by many of his peers.

LECTURE II
CIRCUMSCRIPTION
OF THE TOPIC

2:1 Personal Religion

In these lectures I propose to ignore the institutional branch entirely, to say nothing of the ecclesiastical organization, to consider as little as possible the systematic theology and the ideas about the gods themselves, and to confine myself as far as I can to personal religion pure and simple.

In one sense at least the personal religion will prove itself more fundamental than either theology or ecclesiasticism. Churches, when once established, live at second-hand upon tradition; but the *founders* of every church owed their power originally to the fact of their direct personal communion with the divine. Not only the superhuman founders, the Christ, the Buddha, Mahomet, but all the originators of Christian sects have been in this case; so personal religion should still seem the primordial thing, even to those who continue to esteem it incomplete.

2:1

Here is the heart of what I am calling James's "revolution" in religious studies. I completed a four-year program at a divinity school, but at no point did we discuss the "direct personal communion with the divine" that marks the beginning of all the great sacred traditions. We did not study the nature of religious experience itself. We spent our time with the texts, creeds, and rituals that are in every case derivative products of those founding experiences.

James looks at religion neither with the eyes of the sociologist nor with the eyes of the theologian. Part of the greatness of his work lies precisely in the narrowness of his focus. He doesn't want to hear about the believer's place of worship or the content of his ritual; he has no interest in the believer's catechisms and creeds. With great persistence, James keeps asking one question: what is your personal experience of religion? All the rest is second-hand, belonging more to the group than to the individual.

2:2 RELIGION DEFINED

Religion, therefore, as I now ask you arbitrarily to take it, shall mean for us *the feelings, acts, and experiences of individual men in their solitude, so far as they apprehend themselves to stand in relation to whatever they may consider the divine.*

2:2

People often fail to notice how far removed they are from their religions. Many religious people memorize catechism answers to a multiplicity of questions. Roman Catholics of my generation knew why God made them: "to know, love, and serve God in this life and to be happy with Him in heaven." But we were often at a loss if someone followed up with the more personal question: "What do you believe?" Christians recite creeds in their liturgical services, but not many Christians are ready to write their own creed. And yet, whatever is real for us must ultimately be rooted in our own personal experience. We wouldn't let someone else decide whether or not we liked chocolate cake, whether or not we liked a current movie, whether or not we wanted to wear a sweater today. So why do we let someone or some group speak for us on the most important issue of all: the divine?

It is from this consistently sustained personal focus that James finally produces his definition of religion. Ignoring the community, he looks to the individual with all her feelings, acts, and experiences. And he regards this individual precisely in his relationship to a personal conception of the divine reality. Religion thus conceived entails two premises: that there is something of ultimate importance going on in the universe, and that there is a way of being connected to it.

2:3 ALWAYS MISTY

Solemnity, and gravity, and all such emotional attributes, admit of various shades; and, do what we will with our defining, the truth must at last be confronted that we are dealing with a field of experience where there is not a single conception that can be sharply drawn. The pretension, under such conditions, to be rigorously "scientific" or "exact" in our terms would only stamp us as lacking in understanding of our task. Things are more or less divine, states of mind are more or less religious, reactions are more or less total, but the boundaries are always misty, and it is everywhere a question of amount and degree. Nevertheless, at their extreme of development, there can never be any question as to what experiences are religious.

2:3

It is here that James acknowledges the inevitably subjective dimension of his investigation. Subjectivity, of course, is the bane of the scientific method. Perhaps this is less true in post-Heisenbergian scientific conversation where it is acknowledged that the observer affects the observed, but this insight remains relegated to a handful of philosophers of science. The average scientist is a practitioner, immune to such subtleties.

James realizes the necessity of addressing this head on. There is an expectation of objectivity that cannot be easily transferred, either to the world of the social sciences, or to explorations in the humanities: literature, art, music, and—most importantly for our purposes—religion. This denies neither the rigor of method nor the analysis of evidence; but both method and evidence necessarily have a different meaning in religion than in physics.

2:4 ACCEPTING THE UNIVERSE

At bottom the whole concern of both morality and religion is with the manner of our acceptance of the universe. Do we accept it only in part and grudgingly, or heartily and altogether? Shall our protests against certain things in it be radical and unforgiving, or shall we think that, even with evil, there are ways of living that must lead to good.... Morality pure and simple accepts the law of the whole which it finds reigning, so far as to acknowledge and obey it, but it may obey it with the heaviest and coldest heart, and never cease to feel it as a yoke. But for religion, in its strong and fully developed manifestations, the service of the highest never is felt as a yoke.

2:4

At an unexamined level of awareness, most people think that their emotional reactions are to reality as such. Further examination reveals that our reactions are always to an interpreted reality. To see is to see as. One person may interpret a cloudy day as "nasty weather" while another may interpret it as "a soft old day" (an Irish expression), a good opportunity to snuggle up with that book waiting to be read. Ultimately then we live in a matrix of interpretations, not in a context of naked facts. Religious experience tends to carry with it a certain kind of interpretation of being in the universe. Such an interpretation is not subject to proof or disproof, though one may certainly argue that one interpretation is more persuasive than another.

2:5 SOMEHOW UNIQUE

It is a good rule in physiology, when we are studying the meaning of an organ, to ask after its most peculiar and characteristic sort of performance, and to seek its office in that one of its functions which no other organ can possibly exert. Surely the same maxim holds good in our present quest. The essence of religious experiences, the thing by which we finally must judge them, must be that element or quality in them which we can meet nowhere else.

2:5

What is that quality of religious experience that is met nowhere else? One of the great scholars of world religions, Rudolf Otto, calls it "*das Heilige*," the holy. Just as the world can be seen through the lens of truth, of goodness, or of beauty, so too can it be seen through the lens of holiness. Otto describes the holy as "*mysterium tremendum et fascinans*," a mystery that at once overwhelms us and attracts us. First of all, it is a mystery. It cannot be reduced to a problem to be solved. As a mystery it must be participated in, experienced. Second, it exhibits this paradoxical quality of simultaneously frightening us and drawing us. What do angels say when they appear to mortals? "Do not be afraid." We would certainly be drawn to a manifestation of holiness from a realm beyond ours; and yet, we would understandably be afraid as well.

2:6 An Eternal Present

There is a state of mind, known to religious men, but to no others, in which the will to assert ourselves and hold our own has been displaced by a willingness to close our mouths and be as nothing in the floods and waterspouts of God. In this state of mind, what we most dreaded has become the habitation of our safety, and the hour of our moral death has turned into our spiritual birthday. The time for tension in our soul is over, and that of happy relaxation, of calm deep breathing, of an eternal present, with no discordant future to be anxious about, has arrived. Fear is not held in abeyance as it is by mere morality, it is positively expunged and washed away.

2:6

James addresses this paradoxical reaction to holiness. First of all, the rational, problem-solving mind is silenced. Religious experience exists at a trans-rational level. This is not the same as an irrational or non-rational level, which contradicts reason. These experiences do not fly in the face of reason; they simply elude its grasp. Although the first reaction to such a break-through of holiness might well be a combination of fear and attraction, the fear soon gives way. James states: "...it is positively expunged and washed away."

A classic example of this would be the prophet's Temple vision in the sixth chapter of Isaiah. Seeing the angelic beings and hearing them chant "Holy, holy, holy...," the prophet cries out in anguish and declares that he is lost. But when one of the seraphs cleanses his lips with a live coal from the fire burning at the Temple's altar, Isaiah is ready to become a divine instrument in speaking God's Word to the world. The power of this religious experience catapults him into his challenging mission.

2:7 BEYOND THE RATIONAL

We shall see how infinitely passionate a thing religion at its highest flights can be. Like love, like wrath, like hope, ambition, jealousy, like every other instinctive eagerness and impulse, it adds to life an enchantment which is not rationally or logically deducible from anything else.... Religious feeling is thus an absolute addition to the Subject's range of life. It gives him a new sphere of power. When the outward battle is lost, and the outer world disowns him, it redeems and vivifies an interior world which otherwise would be an empty waste.

2:7

The "outward battle" is the day-to-day struggle with circumstances waged by most human beings. The "interior world" is the world of interpretation. It constitutes a tremendous breakthrough when we realize that our happiness is not defined by our circumstances but by the way in which we interpret them. This opens up a vast field of freedom, but one of responsibility as well. We can no longer play the victim role, asserting that circumstances beyond our control have defeated us. Those circumstances await our interpretation. The *Dhammapada,* an ancient Buddhist text, begins with the assertion that our life follows our thoughts (i.e., interpretation) the way the cart follows the oxen that pull it. There are circumstances we simply cannot change, but there is never a circumstance we cannot interpret.

2:8 RELIGIOUS HAPPINESS

This sort of happiness in the absolute and everlasting is what we find nowhere but in religion. It is parted off from all mere animal happiness, all mere enjoyment of the present, by that element of solemnity of which I have already made so much account.... But such a straight identification of religion with any and every form of happiness leaves the essential peculiarity of religious happiness out.... In its most characteristic embodiments, religious happiness is no mere feeling of escape.

2:8

The recognition that interpretation lives between circumstance and response is not an escape from reality but a doorway to understanding it more profoundly. A friend and colleague of mine was diagnosed with cancer. He was middle-aged, a writer and teacher. In our first phone conversation about this diagnosis, he said to me: "I am praying to know what I should be learning from this." The subsequent path of the illness led to his very painful death. He saw this pain-filled progression of the disease as a "dark night of the soul," a purification of his consciousness before his encounter with God after death. Others would find in these same circumstances nothing more than justifications for bitterness and despair.

2:9 EASY NECESSITY

In the religious life...surrender and sacrifice are positively es-
poused: even unnecessary givings-up are added in order that the
happiness may increase. *Religion thus makes easy and felicitous
what in any case is necessary*; and if it be the only agency that can
accomplish this result, its vital importance as a human faculty
stands vindicated beyond dispute. It becomes an essential organ
of our life, performing a function which no other portion of our
nature can so successfully fulfill.

2:9

Is religion the only agency that can make easy what in any case is necessary? I once heard Viktor Frankel speak. As a young psychiatrist, he was taken to a concentration camp with other Austrian Jews. He witnessed at first hand the different interpretations given by his fellow inmates to this horrible confinement. Some ran against the electric fences in despair; others were willing to sell out their best friends for an extra cigarette; still others prayed each day and lived their lives with dignity and compassion. Frankel was a secular Jew and his motivation was to see his wife again and write a book about his experience. His wife had been killed before his release but he did live to write his book, "Man's Search for Meaning." In it he developed his theory of "logotherapy"— logos (meaning) brings therapy (healing).

Everyone in the camp shared the same basic set of circumstances but each person stood before a variety of interpretations. It's difficult to imagine that any interpretative grid made the horrors of the camp "easy and felicitous," but if they made them somehow bearable, that may have been enough. Not only religion but any overarching goal (such as Frankel's desire to see his wife again or to write his book) could be effective in making life's hard places more bearable. But perhaps James is justified in implying that nothing serves this purpose better than a religious interpretation of reality.

LECTURE III
REALITY OF THE UNSEEN

3:1 Harmonious Adjustment

Were one asked to characterize the life of religion in the broadest and most general terms possible, one might say that it consists of the belief that there is an unseen order, and that our supreme good lies in harmoniously adjusting ourselves thereto.

3:1

This is the critical option. If life is essentially absurd, without purpose or meaning, then no unseen order exists to which we can align ourselves. But if there is a Tao, if the Torah or the Qur'an lays out a template of meaning, if the way of the Buddha or the way of the Christ is compelling, then there is indeed an unseen order and nothing can be more important than living in harmony with it. To move in the rhythm of the Tao, to embody the Torah or the Qur'an, to live as Jesus lived and loved, to follow the path of the Buddha—these alignments, it can be argued, open up for human beings the fullest and most abundant life.

This is the deepest mystery of the great traditions, to offer a way whereby disciples can in some way experience in their own lives what the enlightened teacher experienced in his. Each of these sacred paths invites the initiate to a triple transformation: of consciousness, of conscience, and of community. One sees the world with "the Buddha mind" or "the mind of Christ"; one acts in the world in ways of justice and compassion; one is drawn to new bonds of community—a Sufi circle, a Buddhist *sangha*, a Jewish *chavura*, a Quaker meeting of Friends.

3:2 WARM AND COLD FAITH

We may now lay it down as certain that in the distinctively religious sphere of experience, many persons (how many we cannot tell) possess the objects of their belief, not in the form of mere conceptions which their intellect accepts as true, but rather in the form of quasi-sensible realities directly apprehended. As his sense of the real presence of these objects fluctuates, so the believer alternates between warmth and coldness in his faith.

3:2

James constantly moves his audience from the coldly conceptual world of abstractions to the hot world of experience. As Kierkegaard, the great 19th century philosopher and religious thinker once said: "Christianity is not to think a great thought but to risk a great love." And the same is true for any authentic spiritual path. Religion for James does not primarily reside in belief systems, catechism answers, or orthodox propositions, but in lived experience.

Imagine a friend showing you a classic car in his driveway. The well-polished car gleams in the sunlight. But when you ask to see how the car performs on the road, your friend informs you that it has no engine but is only a chassis. This is the state of religion for many people. They can argue for their cherished dogmas, squabble about liturgical minutiae, point with pride to their new church, synagogue, or mosque. But none of this has effected a transformation in their lives. Their religion has no engine; it is only a chassis. Their faith is cold, however heated their polemics.

3:3 REASON'S CRITERIA

Rationalism insists that all our beliefs ought ultimately to find for themselves articulate grounds. Such grounds, for rationalism, must consist of four things: (1) definitely statable abstract principles; (2) definite facts of sensation; (3) definite hypotheses based on such facts; and (4) definite inferences logically drawn. Vague impressions of something indefinable have no place in the rationalistic system, which on its positive side is surely a splendid intellectual tendency, for not only are all our philosophies fruits of it, but physical science (amongst other good things) is its result.

3:3

Three types of people stand out on our contemporary landscape. There are the scientific fundamentalists (many of the new atheists, such as Christopher Hitchens and Sam Harris) who ask us to choose science and reject religion in all its forms. Then there are the religious fundamentalists (we find them in all the religions) who claim that religion trumps science in every instance. And finally there are those who choose both religion and science, knowing when it is appropriate to solve a problem and when it is time to participate in a mystery.

Both types of fundamentalists are guilty of methodological monism, the belief that there is only one way of knowing reality. Scientism (not science) adheres to the criteria of reason (described here by James) as the only method of finding truth. Religious fundamentalism clings to a literal understanding of their faith that eschews all dialogue with any other way of knowing. James urges us to a balanced approach to knowing the world. One can be both scientist and mystic, physicist and poet, biologist and lover.

LECTURE III

3:4 REASON'S LIMITS

If we look on man's whole mental life as it exists, on the life of men that lies in them apart from their learning and science, and that they inwardly and privately follow, we have to confess that the part of it of which rationalism can give an account is relatively superficial.... If you have intuitions at all, they come from a deeper level of your nature than the loquacious level which rationalism inhabits. Your whole subconscious life, your impulses, your faiths, your needs, your divinations, have prepared the premises, of which your consciousness now feels the weight of the result; and something in you absolutely *knows* that that result must be truer than any logic-chopping rationalistic talk, however clever, that may contradict it.

3:4

I remember a professor of "Psychology of the Child" describing a variety of schools of thought on the subject of early childhood. He had earlier mentioned having several young children himself. One student asked: "When you go home and your children come to greet you, which school of thought do you find most helpful in meeting them?" The teacher laughed and said: "I just hug my children; any school of thought would just get in the way."

One philosopher quipped that most of the "reasons" we give people for our decisions are created after we have already made up our minds. I remember a talk by the great 20th century theologian, Karl Rahner, in which he listed various reasons why one might want to become a Jesuit. When asked why he joined the Jesuits, he smiled and said: "I think it was mainly because my older brother was a Jesuit." As James so aptly remarks, rationalism is found in much of what we *say* ("the loquacious level") but other forces inform most of what we *do*.

LECTURE III

3:5 REASON'S DEFEAT

The unreasoned and immediate assurance is the deep thing in us, the reasoned argument is but a surface exhibition. Instinct leads, intelligence does but follow. If a person feels the presence of a living God...your critical arguments, be they never so superior, will vainly set themselves to change his faith.

3:5

Attempts to prove or disprove God ultimately fail, for the divine is a mystery to be experienced, not a problem to be solved. A faculty colleague of mine once informed me that he was an atheist. I asked him what it would take for him to change his mind. He informed me that he would need a scientific proof of God. I then pointed out that this entailed confusion in our ways of knowing. This colleague was clearly a "methodological monist," believing that all truth could be found through one methodology.

Attempting to open up his reality to other ways of knowing, I suggested that, if he wanted to participate in the divine mystery, he might take a sabbatical to live in a monastery. There he might learn to meditate, chant sacred texts, spend long times in silence and in communion with nature. He just might then experience that dimension of holiness described by Rudolf Otto. He might come to know what Otto called "the numinous." The Latin *numen* refers not to the divine in personal form (as *deus* or *dea*) but as inhabiting nature. The root "*nu*" means "to wave at or nod." It's as though the mystery hidden in the world sometimes tries to catch our attention by waving at us. The Irish call these "thin spaces," places where the mystery is more visible.

LECTURES IV AND V
THE RELIGION OF HEALTHY-MINDEDNESS

4/5:1 Happiness as Proof

How to gain, how to keep, how to recover happiness, is in fact for most men at all times the secret motive of all they do, and of all they are willing to endure…. It is perhaps not surprising that men come to regard the happiness which a religious belief affords as a proof of its truth. If a creed makes a man feel happy, he almost inevitably adopts it.

4/5:1

Philosophers and religious thinkers from Aristotle to the Dalai Lama claim that all human beings desire to be happy. Even when we engage in self-destructive behavior we do it under some pretext of future happiness. The addict taking the next hit hopes that this one will deliver the satisfaction he seeks. James is a pragmatist, realizing that most human beings are not masochists. In religion, as in other areas of life, people tend towards a belief that makes them feel happy.

These observations by James have often been challenged. They seem to suggest that the truth of a religion is irrelevant. As long as the belief makes you feel good, adopt it. Since James is writing about religious experience, he might have made his point more effectively if he had written: "If a religious experience makes a man happy, he almost inevitably adopts it." But perhaps James is simply observing that many people adopt a religion, not on the basis of personal experience, but simply because the belief system of that religion appeals to them. In that case, James is not giving his stamp of approval to this method of making decisions.

4/5:2 EVIL'S ORIGIN

Much of what we call evil is due entirely to the way men take the phenomenon. It can so often be converted into a bracing and tonic good by a simple change of the sufferer's inner attitude from one of fear to one of fight; its sting so often departs and turns into a relish when, after vainly seeking to shun it, we agree to face about and bear it cheerfully, that a man is simply bound in honor, with reference to many of the facts that seem at first to disconcert his peace, to adopt this way of escape. Refuse to admit their badness; despise their power; ignore their presence; turn your attention the other way; and so far as you yourself are concerned at any rate, though the facts may still exist, their evil character exists no longer. Since you make them evil or good by your own thoughts about them, it is the ruling of your thoughts which proves to be your principal concern.

4/5:2

James here broaches the most challenging topic in religious discourse, the presence of evil in the world, the suffering of the innocent, bad things happening to good people. This passage does not claim to give an answer to this profound mystery of human experience but it does offer an important reminder. As we saw earlier, our reality is always an interpreted reality. Evil, therefore, does not exist as some kind of substance, object, or thing. We *call* things evil. Evil resides in a judgment we make, an interpretation.

There is a story in the world of Eastern Jewry in which a poor farmer inherits a horse from a relative. "What good news!" exclaims his neighbor. The man replies: "But my son was riding the horse when he fell off and broke his leg." "What bad news!" exclaims his neighbor. "Yes, but the Czar's agents were recruiting soldiers, and my son couldn't be taken because his leg was broken," says the farmer. "What good news!" exclaims his neighbor. The point of the story is clear. Exactly when and where do we want to insert the judgment that something is bad or good news?

4/5:3 A MANY-SIDED UNIVERSE

The experiences which we have been studying during this hour… plainly show the universe to be a more many-sided affair than any sect, even the scientific sect, allows for. What, in the end, are all our verifications but experiences that agree with more or less isolated systems of ideas (conceptual systems) that our minds have framed? But why in the name of common sense need we assume that only one such system of ideas can be true? The obvious outcome of our total experience is that the world can be handled according to many systems of ideas.

4/5:3

James urges his listeners to a profound humility in the face of life's great mysteries: God, evil, the self, ultimate reality. In another book, James asserts that perhaps in the long run we are in this universe as our cats are in our libraries! It is clearly arrogant to believe that one has a closed system into which all the mysteries of life can be fit. Fundamentalisms of any kind seem naively narrow. Can all truth reside in one book, be it the Bible or the Qur'an? Or can all truth reside in one philosophy, one rational system, one scientific theory? Can all truth be discoverable by one and only one methodology?

4/5:4 BOTH-AND

Science gives to all of us telegraphy, electric lighting, and diagnosis, and succeeds in preventing and curing a certain amount of disease. Religion in the shape of mind-cure gives to some of us serenity, moral poise, and happiness, and prevents certain forms of disease as well as science does, or even better in a certain class of persons. Evidently, then, the science and the religion are both of them genuine keys for unlocking the world's treasure-house to him who can use either of them practically.

4/5:4

Rejecting both religious fundamentalism and scientific fundamentalism, James offers us a third way. There are problems best addressed by the scientific method. There are mysteries, however, which can only be experienced by the methods of religion and spiritual practice. Why do people feel compelled to an either-or view of truth?

There are levels of consciousness and various thinkers offer maps of this terrain. We can distinguish, for example, one-narrative consciousness from rational consciousness and rational consciousness from the trans-rational consciousness of mystics. The one-narrative mind recognizes only one account of reality, one avenue to truth. James invites us to a higher consciousness where we can be in dialogue with another narrative, another account of reality, another avenue to truth.

LECTURES VI AND VII
THE SICK SOUL

6/7:1 The Sick Soul's Disease

Evil is a disease; and worry over disease is itself an additional form of disease, which only adds to the original complaint. Even repentance and remorse, affections which come in the character of ministers of good, may be but sickly and relaxing impulses. The best repentance is to up and act for righteousness, and forget that you ever had relations with sin.

6/7:1

There is a human tendency to compound our problems by worrying about them. The worry or anxiety is not a productive response to the problem. James argues that when confronting evil in one's own past choices, it is healthier not to obsess over these past mistakes but to learn from them and then stand up and act for righteousness.

When people stew in their mistakes, they end up only compounding them. Using their energies in trying to recreate a past that cannot be altered, they are left powerless to choose and create a future that can be realized.

6/7:2 LEVELS OF EVIL

Just as we saw that in healthy-mindedness there are shallower and profounder levels, happiness like that of the mere animal, and more regenerate sorts of happiness, so also are there different levels of the morbid mind, and the one is much more formidable than the other. There are people for whom evil means only a mal-adjustment with things, a wrong correspondence of one's life with the environment. Such evil as this is curable, in principle at least, upon the natural plane, for merely by modifying either the self or the things, or both at once, the two terms may be made to fit, and all go merry as a marriage bell again. But there are others for whom evil is no mere relation of the subject to particular outer things, but something more radical and general, a wrongness or vice in his essential nature, which no alteration of the environment, or any superficial rearrangement of the inner self, can cure, and which requires a supernatural remedy.

6/7:2

Here James acknowledges different levels of health and sickness. Some can be healthy-minded simply because they have not experienced much of the world's problems. Others can be sick souls because they have never moved beyond the narrow confines of some early negative impressions of the world. But there is a more mature form of healthy-mindedness that has seen evil and yet affirms the good, what the poet Hopkins calls "the dearest freshness deep down things." And there are more mature sick souls who have seen the goodness of life and yet find that the overwhelming presence of evil tends to blot out every ray of sunshine.

My criticism of James here is two-fold. First, the two categories (sick and healthy) are too simplistic. A spectrum running from sick to healthy would serve his purposes better. Second, there should be a recognition of the degree of maturity one has in her particular point on the spectrum. In other words, a sick soul at sixteen would normally manifest different characteristics than a sick soul at sixty, who had spent forty years in a monastic setting of prayer and meditation.

6/7:3 DIFFERENT RELIGIOUS NEEDS

Does it not appear as if one who lived more habitually on one side of the pain-threshold might need a different sort of religion from one who habitually lived on the other? This question, of the relativity of different types of religion to different types of need, arises naturally at this point.

6/7:3

Because James is regarding religion from the vantage point of subjective experience, not of objective dogmas, it makes sense that one person's religion will differ from another's. In fact, since religion encompasses the subjectivity of human experience, each person's religion is in some way as unique as the individual. I once heard a noted rabbi remark that to be a Jew is to have a covenant with God, but that there may not be any two Jews with the same covenant.

This presents a challenge to religion that it seems to me is seldom recognized and even more rarely addressed. In a chemistry lab, everyone is supposed to come up with the same results. But should this be true of religion? The Sunday sermon is often a "one size fits all" phenomenon. But do some of the congregants need to be challenged, while others need comforting? And how can one sermon do both? Perhaps some members of the congregation require a meditative, contemplative form of worship, while others respond to an energetic, hand-clapping meeting. Can one service adequately meet both needs?

6/7:4 DELIVERANCE

Provisionally, and as a mere matter of program and method, since the evil facts are as genuine parts of nature as the good ones, the philosophic presumption should be that they have some rational significance, and that systematic healthy-mindedness, failing as it does to accord to sorrow, pain, and death any positive and active attention whatever, is formally less complete than systems that try at least to include these elements in their scope. The completest religions would therefore seem to be those in which the pessimistic elements are best developed. Buddhism, of course, and Christianity are the best known to us of these. They are essentially religions of deliverance: the man must die to an unreal life before he can be born into the real life.

6/7:4

At this point I find James inconsistent. If both types are equally valid, why are we now informed that the most complete forms of religion are those that meet the needs of the sick souls? He seems to be saying that healthy-mindedness cannot reach the finish line. It must merge at some point into the lane defined by the sick soul. Familiarity with James's biography reveals our thinker as a classic sick soul. It seems unavoidable that this personal experience would color his reading of the testimony of others.

James asserts that the most complete religions are those which are "religions of deliverance," epitomized most clearly by Buddhism and Christianity. Such a judgment makes clear sense from the perspective of a sick soul, whereas a healthy-minded soul would find such completeness without a theology of deliverance. This is yet another example of his own personal bias.

My final observation on this portion of the text is that, as I mentioned earlier, his dichotomous characterization of the soul is ultimately too simplistic. His schema would be more effective if it were a spectrum of personality types stretching from healthy to sick. Such a spectrum should also allow for different levels of maturity within a given type. Although this introduces a greater complexity into the discussion, it nevertheless provides for a more sophisticated understanding of a particular religious personality.

LECTURE VIII
THE DIVIDED SELF, AND THE PROCESS OF ITS UNIFICATION

8:1 CHAOS TO UNIFICATION

Now in all of us, however constituted, but to a degree the greater in proportion as we are intense and sensitive and subject to diversified temptations, and to the greatest possible degree if we are decidedly psychopathic, does the normal evolution of character chiefly consist in the straightening out and unifying of the inner self. The higher and the lower feelings, the useful and the erring impulses, begin by being a comparative chaos within us—they must end by forming a stable system of functions in right subordination.

8:1

Incoherence throws up a red flag for most psychiatrists. Psychological growth tends towards coherence. Kierkegaard claimed that purity of heart means to will one thing. In other words, despite the diverse tasks facing mature people, their lives move towards a coherent pattern. And despite the conflict of emotions and tendencies in any normal person, a stable system begins to emerge with psychological growth. Priorities tend to remain priorities and secondary forces remain subordinate. James is giving us some preliminary background for discussing the experience of a divided self and the process of its unification.

8:2 RELIGION'S POWER

Happiness! happiness! religion is only one of the ways in which men gain that gift. Easily, permanently, and successfully, it often transforms the most intolerable misery into the profoundest and most enduring happiness.

But to find religion is only one out of many ways of reaching unity; and the process of remedying inner incompleteness and reducing inner discord is a general psychological process, which may take place with any sort of mental material, and need not necessarily assume the religious form.

8:2

Religion is one of the ways in which a divided self can become whole. And with wholeness comes happiness. The sense of life's energies leaking out through gaps of the soul tends to debilitate and discourage people. But when unity is achieved and life's energies are drawn together towards a goal, the soul leaps forward with vigor and alacrity.

Mystical consciousness (which we will say more about later) provides the greatest experience of unity and it is therefore not surprising that mystics exhibit remarkable energy. They are not wasting any of their energy along deviant paths and thus we see in them a focus, an attention, and a profound sense of presence.

LECTURE IX
CONVERSION

9:1 Transformation

Our ordinary alterations of character, as we pass from one of our aims to another, are not commonly called transformations, because each of them is so rapidly succeeded by another in the reverse direction; but whenever one aim grows so stable as to expel definitively its previous rivals from the individual's life, we tend to speak of the phenomenon, and perhaps to wonder at it, as a "transformation."

9:1

Not every change entails instant transformation. Some changes are incremental; others represent a back and forth movement between opposite forces. To practice daily and slowly become a better violinist would constitute an incremental change, the more common form of human experience. But a profound change, one that thoroughly replaces one kind of character with another, merits being called a transformation. This parallels a "paradigm shift" in science, for instance from a geocentric to a heliocentric view of our solar system. If you move from casual playing of the violin to the passionate determination to be a concert violinist, that exemplifies what James means by a transformation.

9:2 HOT AND COLD

As life goes on, there is a constant change of our interests, and a consequent change of place in our systems of ideas, from more central to more peripheral, and from more peripheral to more central parts of consciousness.... What brings such changes about is the way in which emotional excitement alters. Things hot and vital to us to-day are cold to-morrow. It is as if seen from the hot parts of the field that the other parts appear to us, and from these hot parts personal desire and volition make their sallies. They are in short the centres of our dynamic energy, whereas the cold parts leave us indifferent and passive in proportion to their coldness.

9:2

James's use of hot and cold parts of our field of consciousness reminds me of my experience many years ago in my aunt's kitchen. I spent part of every summer on her farm where she had the task of preparing food for family, guests, and farm hands…a full table of some twelve hungry people. She cooked at a large wood-burning stove and one of my chores as a boy was bringing in the buckets of dried corncobs used for fuel.

I watched with wonder as my aunt coordinated the cooking process for the diverse foods to be served up for our consumption. Something needing more heat was pulled towards the center of the stove's surface; something just needing to stay warm was moved to the periphery. So it is with consciousness. Something heating up too quickly may be pushed away from the heat to cool down a bit, while something sitting on the cooler periphery may need to be pulled to the place of greatest heat.

9:3 FROM PERIPHERY TO CENTRE

Let us hereafter, in speaking of the hot place in a man's consciousness, the group of ideas to which he devotes himself, and from which he works, call it *the habitual centre of his personal energy*. It makes a great difference to a man whether one set of his ideas, or another, be the centre of his energy; and it makes a great difference, as regards any set of ideas which he may possess, whether they become central or remain peripheral in him. To say that a man is "converted" means, in these terms, that religious ideas, previously peripheral in his consciousness, now take a central place, and that religious aims form the habitual centre of his energy.

9:3

James can now speak of someone's habitual center of personal energy, the hot place in someone's consciousness. The name given to this shift from cold to hot is conversion. The idea of conversion is not limited to religious consciousness. If you attend a concert and are fascinated by the violinist and then develop such a passion for the violin that you can settle for nothing less than practicing eight hours a day, you have experienced a conversion. So the process can be similar, while the content can vary. But when the content is religious, so too is the conversion.

I remember a lecture during my first year in the seminary. The speaker was Fr. Robert North, S.J., a distinguished scholar from the Gregorian University in Rome. He spoke on the books of Ezra and Nehemiah, hardly the high points of the Hebrew Bible. Nevertheless, I was captivated by his presentation and knew that I wanted to study and teach the Bible for the rest of my days. Up until then, I had regarded the Bible as a rather dry source of proof texts for theological propositions; but after that day it was a magnet that drew me. That shift was a personal conversion.

9:4 EXPLANATION FAILS

Now if you ask of psychology just *how* the excitement shifts in a man's mental system, and *why* aims that were peripheral become at a certain moment central, psychology has to reply that although she can give a general description of what happens, she is unable in a given case to account accurately for all the single forces at work. Neither an outside observer nor the Subject who undergoes the process can explain fully how particular experiences are able to change one's centre of energy so decisively, or why they so often have to bide their hour to do so.

9:4

My experience at Fr. Robert North's lecture occurred more than fifty years ago, and to this day I cannot explain it. Why do I remember where I was sitting in the auditorium? Why do I remember going to my room afterwards and picking up the Bible with a new-found curiosity? Learning Hebrew and Greek, taking numerous courses in pursuing a graduate degree in theology, reading and writing on biblical topics to this day, teaching the Bible at every opportunity…all of this became easy and attractive. The hot center had been found.

This is an exciting but ultimately unfathomable part of human experience. My son received a drum set as one of his Christmas presents when he was about twelve years old. From the moment he first made a sound on those drums, he was a drummer. A series of bands followed, hours of practice, club shows, relocation in Los Angeles, vibrant center of the music he still loves. It was all there, like the oak tree in the acorn, from the day he first sat down at that miniature drum set that Christmas morning many years ago. He had experienced a conversion.

9:5 IMPERVIOUS TO CONVERSION

Some persons, for instance, never are, and possibly never under any circumstances could be, converted. Religious ideas cannot become the centre of their spiritual energy.... They are either incapable of imagining the invisible; or else, in the language of devotion, they are life-long subjects of "barrenness" and "dryness." Such inaptitude for religious faith may in some cases be intellectual in its origin. Their religious faculties may be checked in their natural tendency to expand, by beliefs about the world that are inhibitive, the pessimistic and materialistic beliefs, for example, within which so many good souls, who in former times would have freely indulged their religious propensities, find themselves nowadays, as it were, frozen; or the agnostic vetoes... faith as something weak and shameful.... In many persons such inhibitions are never overcome. To the end of their days they refuse to believe, their personal energy never gets to its religious centre, and the latter remains inactive in perpetuity.

9:5

As obvious as a conversion experience is to the one who has it, it often remains incomprehensible to the one looking on from a distance. A noted sociologist once said that religion was a music for which he simply didn't have the ear. Spending years with the Bible would be a torture for many people, just as drumming holds no appeal for countless others.

James suggests that the "inaptitude for religious faith" might in some cases have an intellectual origin. I remember sitting on a thesis defense committee with an undergrad who defined himself as a secular humanist. I asked him how he would react if he were sitting outside one day and was suddenly hit by an oceanic wave of mystical consciousness, finding himself suffused with a sense of union with everyone and everything and weeping with a boundless sense of love and compassion. He looked at me somewhat puzzled and said that he would immediately go and see his doctor and try to find out what kind of chemical imbalance produced this aberration. He did not seem to be a likely candidate for a religious conversion. Or perhaps, for precisely this reason, he was.

9:6 SELF-SURRENDER

Of the volitional type of conversion it would be easy to give examples, but they are as a rule less interesting than those of the self-surrender type, in which the subconscious effects are more abundant and often startling. I will therefore hurry to the latter, the more so because the difference between the two types is after all not radical. Even in the most voluntarily built-up sort of regeneration there are passages of partial self-surrender interposed; and in the great majority of all cases, when the will had done its uttermost towards bringing one close to the complete unification aspired after, it seems that the very last step must be left to other forces and performed without the help of its activity.

9:6

James touches here upon a topic that in some religious conversations is called "grace." Although human volition may well be involved, what predominates seems to be a gift. Judaism speaks of the "*matan Torah*," the gift of the Torah, implying that Moses *received* the Torah; he didn't wrestle it from God's hands. The experience of Siddhartha Gotama under the tree led to his becoming the Buddha, the one who woke up. The narrative suggests that this transformation was a gift, more than the result of a regimen of spiritual practices.

In Jesus's parable of the sower, found in the fourth chapter of Mark (also in Thomas, Matthew, and Luke), the seed sown by the farmer is good, as are the rain and the sunshine. The variable in the story is the soil, rocky or receptive. Some kind of soil receptivity precedes the productive growing of the seed. And yet, there are times when stubborn resistance seems to be the best preparation, like Paul who apparently needed the rather dramatic divine intervention of being knocked off his horse. The law of grace eludes all human logic.

9:7 Faith without Doctrine

One may say that the whole development of Christianity in inwardness has consisted in little more than the greater and greater emphasis attached to this crisis of self-surrender. From Catholicism to Lutheranism, and then to Calvinism; from that to Wesleyanism; and from this, outside of technical Christianity altogether, to pure "liberalism" or transcendental idealism, whether or not of the mind-cure type, taking in the mediaeval mystics, the quietists, the pietists, and quakers by the way, we can trace the stages of progress towards the idea of an immediate spiritual help, experienced by the individual in his forlornness and standing in no essential need of doctrinal apparatus or propitiatory machinery.

9:7

The histories of religion, so popular in the 19th century, often betrayed the prejudices of their authors. The classic products of German scholarship, beginning with Hegel himself, usually traced religion from primitive animism through its evolution to its most "perfect" form: German Protestant Christianity. Today's scholars are more likely to reassess animism as one of the highest forms of pantheistic experience, i.e., the realization that the whole manifold of creation is God in manifest form

James's bias lies in another direction than that of his German counterparts. Lutheranism is but the second rung of his ladder, better only than the Catholicism that preceded it. We climb next to Calvin's reform and on to Methodism, transcendental idealism, mind-cure religions (like Christian Science), the Quakers (and other groups maintaining the mysticism of the Middle Ages), and finally, at the top of the ladder, "the individual in his forlornness" with no need of creed or cult.

Not surprisingly, this brings us back to James's definition of religion: "The feelings, acts, and experiences of individual men in their solitude, so far as they apprehend themselves to stand in relation to whatever they may consider the divine" (2:2). Jewish commentators have often been the most outspoken critics of James's apparent lack of appreciation for the communal dimension of religion, a prime characteristic of Jewish spirituality.

9:8 EGO GUARDS THE DOOR

There are only two ways in which it is possible to get rid of anger, worry, fear, despair, or other undesirable affections. One is that an opposite affection should overpoweringly break over us, and the other is by getting so exhausted with the struggle that we have to stop—so we drop down, give up, and *don't care* any longer. Our emotional brain-centres strike work, and we lapse into a temporary apathy. Now there is documentary proof that this state of temporary exhaustion not infrequently forms part of the conversion crisis. So long as the egoistic worry of the sick soul guards the door, the expansive confidence of the soul of faith gains no presence. But let the former faint away, even but for a moment, and the latter can profit by the opportunity, and, having once acquired possession, may retain it.

9:8

Studies of addiction give clear evidence that some people have to hit bottom before they are open to recovery. I met a teenage girl with an alcohol problem, who was in such deep denial that she had to total three cars, suffer personal physical injury, and finally be jailed for this behavior, before she woke up to the fact that she was an alcoholic. With the help of Alcoholics Anonymous she went on to a healthy and productive life as a recovering alcoholic.

The great medieval mystic from Erfurt, Meister Eckhart, spoke of a *Durchbruch,* a break-through experience. Somehow the "false self" that guards the door to our personal growth must be pushed out of the way before "the expansive confidence of the soul of faith" can acquire possession of the soul. Sometimes this higher consciousness overwhelms us; at other times, we tire of trying to keep it out. In that case, when the false self collapses, exhausted by its own neurotic efforts, the higher consciousness simply climbs over it, successfully taking possession of the soul.

LECTURE X
CONVERSION CONCLUDED

10:1 The Dreamy Subliminal

Just as our primary wide-awake consciousness throws open our senses to the touch of things material so it is logically conceivable that if there be higher spiritual agencies that can directly touch us, the psychological condition of their doing so might be our possession of a subconscious region which alone should yield access to them. The hubbub of the waking life might close a door which in the dreamy Subliminal might remain ajar or open.

10:1

In our ordinary consciousness, waking consciousness, we deal primarily with the physical world around us. But when we recognize a larger spectrum of consciousness, new horizons of potential experience spread out before us. What "spiritual agencies" might meet us there? If the subconscious is the face of God, then what rises from the subconscious might indeed be divine messengers. Synchronicity (those strange coincidences that elude normal causality), dreams, "Freudian slips," somatic symptoms (the "pain in our neck" that may be a metaphor for our boss)... this whole blossoming of life at the level of psychic consciousness follows from our being open to life beyond normal, waking consciousness.

My mother had died some years before, but I woke up one morning thinking of her and remembering that it was her birthday. I addressed her almost jokingly, saying: "I can't get you anything for your birthday, so why don't you surprise me today?" Thinking little more about this, I drove to meet a former student, now friend, who lives in Wisconsin. It was a beautiful day and he suggested we go for a *"Fahrt ins Blau"*...a drive with no destination. I called out for him to stop at one point. There was a road sign with the words: "Alvina's Way." That was my mother's name. I smiled at the synchronicity, just one example of what people so often experience. When we are open to the realm of psychic consciousness, James opines that "higher spiritual agencies" can indeed touch us.

10:2 A High-water Mark

Men lapse from every level—we need no statistics to tell us that. Love is, for instance, well known not to be irrevocable, yet, constant or inconstant, it reveals new flights and reaches of ideality while it lasts. These revelations form its significance to men and women, whatever be its duration. So with the conversion experience: that it should for even a short time show a human being what the high-water mark of his spiritual capacity is, this is what constitutes its importance—an importance which backsliding cannot diminish, although persistence might increase it.

10:2

Breakthroughs are not necessarily permanent. The wisdom of a remembered dream jotted down upon waking may soon be forgotten in the busy-ness of our day, the bills to be paid, the deadlines to be met, the meals to be cooked, the laundry to be folded and put away. When we return to the plains of ordinary consciousness, we can all too easily forget our "peak experiences," what we had learned in the thinner air of our mind mountains, what we had clearly seen in those glimpses of a higher order. But James asserts that these forgotten visions are nonetheless not forever wasted. What met us once may return another day. Just as our muscles have memory, so to do our souls. Something we have no need for today may be there for a later day when we require it.

Nevertheless, it would be better for us to increase this mountaintop vision through persistence, rather than take the risk of losing it through backsliding. This opens up the path of practice and leads us to the discussion of saintliness. When asked for the essential ingredient for becoming a saint, Thomas Aquinas responded with one word: "*Velle!*" Will it! Want it! So simple and yet so difficult. For it's a long road from a velleity to a volition, from the subjunctive mood (I would like that) to the indicative mood (I want it). It is the path of practice, of spiritual discipline, and of asceticism.

LECTURES XI, XII, XIII
SAINTLINESS

11/12/13:1 SAINTLINESS

The collective name for the ripe fruits of religion in a character is Saintliness. The saintly character is the character for which spiritual emotions are the habitual centre of the personal energy; and there is a certain composite photograph of universal saintliness, the same in all religions, of which the features can easily be traced.

11/12/13:1

The great saints, the exemplars, the holy people in all the sacred traditions of the world, have one very important thing in common. They have all experienced a religious conversion, whether early or late in life. And this means that spiritual emotions regularly reside on the hottest place in their field of consciousness. James asserts that one result of this is a composite portrait of saintliness exhibiting many of the same central traits.

Others have pursued this project and the result is indeed a kind of composite picture of saintliness. The characteristics I would choose are not identical with the ones James chose but they are similar enough to demonstrate that James stands at the source of this investigation. I find in these figures a sustained peace of soul and an abiding joy. Accompanying this is a great wisdom, an ability to see diverse elements in a coordinated vision. Present too is a deep sense of compassion, of unconditional positive regard for others without barriers or boundaries. To all of this is joined a profound humility, a groundedness in truth. Unlike the anxious proselytizers who populate the world of religion, these giants have nothing to prove and nothing to defend. They take themselves lightly and readily laugh at themselves, eschewing any pretense of being other than ordinary.

11/12/13:2 ENLARGERS OF OUR LIFE

A feeling of being in a wider life than that of this world's selfish little interests; and a conviction, not merely intellectual, but as it were sensible, of the existence of an Ideal Power. In Christian saintliness this power is always personified as God; but abstract moral ideals, civic or patriotic utopias, or inner versions of holiness or right may also be felt as the true lords and enlargers of our life, in ways which I described in the lecture on the Reality of the Unseen.

11/12/13:2

These exemplars of religion inhabit a larger world. Since our world consists of our interpretation of our circumstances, and since our interpretation forms our consciousness, saints clearly have a larger consciousness than most human beings. Christians call this "the mind of Christ," as Buddhists refer to it as "Buddha mind." In Jewish mysticism this is a consciousness that is "*gadlut*," big; and a Hindu possessed of this consciousness merits being called "Mahatma," big self. This transformation of consciousness from little to big characterizes all the sacred traditions.

This difference in size of one's inhabited world is not merely a truth to be acknowledged, but a practice to be incorporated into one's own life. A woman came to me once, worried about the upcoming Thanksgiving holiday. The family gathering inevitably pitted her against a rival relative who delighted in tormenting her. A typical greeting might be: "Darling, you look just as nice in that dress as you have for the last five Thanksgivings on which you have worn it." What could she do? I asked her to choose her favorite spiritual model. She chose the Buddha. I suggested that she imagine herself inhabiting the body of the Buddha and try to meet this other as the Buddha. She came back a week later with a smile on her face. "The Buddha handled it perfectly," she said. "I realized that whatever she was saying had nothing to do with me and let her words pass over me like clouds over my head. It was my best Thanksgiving ever."

11/12/13:3 ASCETICISM

The self-surrender may become so passionate as to turn into self-immolation. It may then so over-rule the ordinary inhibitions of the flesh that the saint finds positive pleasure in sacrifice and asceticism, measuring and expressing as they do the degree of his loyalty to the higher power.

11/12/13:3

James correctly identifies a characteristic pattern of bodily mortification as part of the profile of many saints. I omit it, however, from my list, since asceticism seems all too often rooted in a philosophy that downplays or even denies the essential goodness of our bodily existence. We see this especially in some forms of Hinduism and Christianity. I refer to this as the path of "holy abstinence." The way to the divine is conceived as a ladder climbing up from the world of matter. The more we abstain from bodily existence, the closer we move to the divine.

In contrast to this, some of the traditions encourage a path of moderation, what I call a "blessed participation" in the world. Avoiding the extremes both of asceticism and hedonism, one participates in the pleasures of the world with gratitude and moderation. The Buddha encouraged this path. We find it too in Judaism, Islam, and the religions of China. The Jewish philosopher and religious thinker, Martin Buber, asserted that the world was not an obstacle on the way to God but instead *was* the way. Put another way, we are not human beings learning to be spiritual, but spiritual beings learning to be human. To deny our human existence is to reject the path of growth laid out before us.

11/12/13:4 PURITY

The shifting of the emotional centre brings with it, first, increase of purity. The sensitiveness to spiritual discords is enhanced, and the cleansing of existence from brutal and sensual elements becomes imperative. Occasions of contact with such elements are avoided: the saintly life must deepen its spiritual consistency and keep unspotted from the world. In some temperaments this need of purity of spirit takes an ascetic turn, and weaknesses of the flesh are treated with relentless severity.

11/12/13:4

What does it mean to be "unspotted from the world"? I would reject any interpretation of this phrase that seeks to deny either the goodness of the physical world or the importance of our joyful and grateful participation in that world. On the other hand, addiction and enslavement to the pleasures of life in the world are clearly not conducive to spiritual growth. They are rightly to be condemned. In this case, the "world" is best understood as "worldliness" or a bondage to the world that blots out the face of God and of our neighbor.

The world of nature, the world of shared food and drink, the world of human intimacy—this is a world to be embraced and enjoyed. But when participation leads to greed, when enjoyment becomes addiction, when intimacy becomes exploitation, then there emerges a "world" we must mightily reject. But the lives of the saints, especially in the Christian tradition, suggest that this distinction is sometimes blurred. What results is a world-hating abstinence, a form of "Puritanism" that robs human beings of the joys of blessed participation.

11/12/13:5 The Other Kingdom

Psychologically and in principle, the precept "Love your enemies" is not self-contradictory. It is merely the extreme limit of a kind of magnanimity with which, in the shape of pitying tolerance of our oppressors, we are fairly familiar. Yet if radically followed, it would involve such a breach with our instinctive springs of action as a whole, and with the present world's arrangements, that a critical point would practically be passed, and we should be born into another kingdom of being. Religious emotion makes us feel that other kingdom to be close at hand, within our reach.

11/12/13:5

The challenge to "love our enemies" can perhaps best be understood within a framework of stages of consciousness. Thinking of consciousness as a house we inhabit, one-narrative consciousness is its basement, rational consciousness its first floor, psychic consciousness its second floor, and mystical consciousness its roof deck. At the one-narrative level, we hate our enemies and seek to destroy them. At the rational level, we negotiate with them and are open to understanding the validity of their narrative. At the psychic level, we begin to feel from the other side, from the lived experience of those we call our enemies. But surely it is only from the mystical level of consciousness, transcending any kind of dualism, that we can love our enemies.

Many people now and then experience a glimpse of that mystical consciousness, but only the saints inhabit it as their habitual way of seeing the world. Through this radical transformation of consciousness, these saints have indeed been born into what James calls "another kingdom of being." They live in a world most of us cannot understand. Gandhi, seeing the assassin aiming a gun at him, bows and says the name of God: Rama. Jesus prays for the Roman soldiers nailing him to the wood of the cross: "Father, forgive them; they don't know what they are doing" (Luke 23:34).

11/12/13:6 REMOVING THE YOKE

The transition from tenseness, self-responsibility, and worry, to equanimity, receptivity, and peace, is the most wonderful of all those shiftings of inner equilibrium, those changes of the personal centre of energy, which I have analyzed so often; and the chief wonder of it is that it so often comes about, not by doing, but by simply relaxing and throwing the burden down. This abandonment of self-responsibility seems to be the fundamental act in specifically religious, as distinguished from moral practice.

11/12/13:6

What is the burden that James asserts the saints are able to let go of and throw down? It is the burden of a life centered on a false sense of self, a life focused on the needs and desires of the ego. The spiritual teacher and mystic, Krishnamurti, was once asked how it was that he was able to be happy all the time. He responded: "Because I don't care what happens to me." In other words, he didn't care what happened to his "small" self. We could find no clearer articulation of the point James is making. Krishnamurti had indeed let go of the burden of a life centered on that false and all too limited self.

The larger self is God-centered. In Biblical language, this is what is meant by being "righteous" or "justified." One's life is centered in the larger self. And since the larger self is the divine reality, it cannot be threatened by any external agent. As Paul writes in Romans 8:38-39: "I am convinced that neither death, nor life, nor angels, nor rulers, nor things present, nor things to come, nor powers, nor height, nor depth, nor anything else in all creation, will be able to separate us from the love of God in Christ Jesus our Lord." Like Gandhi, like Krishnamurti, Paul and all the saints live beyond the anxiety of the ultimately fruitless attempt to maintain the false self as the center of one's mental universe.

LECTURES XIV AND XV
THE VALUE OF SAINTLINESS

14/15:1 NOT ONE FOR ALL

Ought all men to have the same religion? Ought they to approve the same fruits and follow the same leadings? Are they so like in their inner needs that, for hard and soft, for proud and humble, for strenuous and lazy, for healthy-minded and despairing, exactly the same religious incentives are required? Or are different functions in the organism of humanity allotted to different types of man, so that some may really be the better for a religion of consolation and reassurance, whilst others are better for one of terror and reproof?

14/15:1

It has been said that a good sermon should both afflict the comfortable and comfort the afflicted. This presents a formidable challenge for any preacher. There is no one pedagogical method that works with all students. Some can learn best by hearing; others by seeing. Some students excel in writing papers but are poor test-takers; other students are the opposite. Religion is a vehicle; its purpose is to lead us to the triple transformation of consciousness, conscience, and community. It is unlikely that any one religion can work best for everyone.

When Swami Vivekenanda was in Chicago for the World's Parliament of Religions in 1893, he remarked that the menu in his hotel restaurant offered a variety of entrées. This led him to reflect on the desirability of having many religions. God is like a mother who spoils her children by cooking for each one his or her favorite dish. Some like best the taste of Judaism, while others prefer Hinduism or Islam or Christianity. It is unlikely that all the hotel guests will order the same entrée. So then why should it surprise us then that human beings find a spiritual home in a variety of traditions?

14/15:2 DOWN ON DOGMA

In critically judging of the value of religious phenomena, it is very important to insist on the distinction between religion as an individual personal function, and religion as an institutional, corporate, or tribal product.... When these groups get strong enough to "organize" themselves, they become ecclesiastical institutions with corporate ambitions of their own. The spirit of politics and the lust of dogmatic rule are then apt to enter and to contaminate the originally innocent thing; so that when we hear the word "religion" nowadays, we think inevitably of some "church" or other; and to some persons the word "church" suggests so much hypocrisy and tyranny and meanness and tenacity of superstition that in a wholesale undiscerning way they glory in saying that they are "down" on religion altogether.

14/15:2

Though written more than a hundred years ago, these words seem uncannily relevant to the lives of so many people today. In my course on "Religion in Contemporary America," I ask students to indicate on a slip of paper the way they would identify themselves in terms of religion. These are done anonymously and then collected. The most common identification of students today is some form of: "spiritual but not religious." There is a clear mistrust of religious organizations. The financial scams of so many televangelists and the sexual scandals among Roman Catholic clergy are certainly part of this picture. And yet, something deeper seems to be playing a role in this growing unwillingness to identify with a religious organization. Young people, and some older ones as well, see all too clearly the tendency of religious organizations to practice self-idolatry. Just as individuals have false selves, so too do institutions.

A Buddhist was speaking to my class one day. He had given a wonderful presentation on meditation and invited student feedback. One student asked about Hindu meditation and the speaker responded that Hindu meditation can serve as a relaxing technique but was incapable of leading to enlightenment. I saw the looks on the faces of the students; they recognized this "car-salesman" approach to religion. What a turn-off for those young minds, and what a short step from rejecting the religious arrogance of the speaker to rejecting religion altogether.

14/15:3 ORTHODOXY

A genuine first-hand religious experience…is bound to be a heterodoxy to its witnesses, the prophet appearing as a mere lonely madman. If his doctrine prove contagious enough to spread to any others, it becomes a definite and labeled heresy. But if it then still prove contagious enough to triumph over persecution, it becomes itself an orthodoxy; and when a religion has become an orthodoxy, its day of inwardness is over: the spring is dry; the faithful live at second hand exclusively and stone the prophets in their turn.

14/15:3

James does not present a very hopeful picture for the development of religion. Orthodoxy is often nothing more than the belief system of the victors in history's religious struggles. Heresy, on the other hand, reveals the belief systems of the losers. The recent discovery of gospels long buried in the sands of Egypt throws new light on how the canon of the Christian Testament was formed in the fourth century. Since the final cut was made by male bishops, it is not surprising that the six gospels attributing leadership to Mary Magdalene were dropped. Restoring the voices and roles of women in Christianity confronts today's churches as a demanding challenge.

How can this oppressive tendency in religion be countered? There needs to be clear channels for prophets to speak to power. The "closed system" model of religion needs to be replaced by the "open-ended conversation." And there must be room for new voices. I recently attended a wonderful conference on "Globalization for the Common Good." One of the highlights of the week was a youth panel. The young voices suggested a total rethinking of many of the structures and practices held dear by the older generation. It was here that the gray-haired leadership could feel the force of future challenging their cherished structures. It is only by this kind of listening that the hardening of religion's arteries described by James can be cured.

14/15:4 RELIGION'S WICKED PARTNERS

The basenesses so commonly charged to religion's account are thus, almost all of them, not chargeable at all to religion proper, but rather to religion's wicked practical partner, the spirit of corporate dominion. And the bigotries are most of them in their turn chargeable to religion's wicked intellectual partner, the spirit of dogmatic dominion, the passion for laying down the law in the form of an absolutely closed-in theoretic system. The ecclesiastical spirit in general is the sum of these two spirits of dominion.

14/15:4

So many of the new atheists writing today fail to recognize the salient point that James is making. What they are criticizing is often, not "religion proper" but its wicked partners. We need always to remember that religion never walks alone. On either side it is accompanied by a powerful presence: "the spirit of corporate dominion" on one side and "the spirit of dogmatic dominion" on the other. In other words, wherever we find religion, it is embedded in a culture, a matrix of interpretations that often has purposes at odds with the religion it purports to embrace. At the same time, religion stands in constant danger of falling under the control of power brokers seeking to control people through religious dogma.

Adherents of religious traditions face the challenge of wrestling religion free from this corporate and dogmatic dominion. In my books about Christianity, I often speak of the quest to find "Jesus without Christianity," in other words, the Galilean wisdom teacher prior to the empire-building conquests in the wake of Constantine's cooptation of Christianity in the 4th century. As the empire increasingly became Christian, so too did Christianity increasingly become imperial. Reversing this trend is no easy matter.

14/15:5 THE MASK OF PIETY

The baiting of Jews, the hunting of Albigenses and Waldenses, the stoning of Quakers and ducking of Methodists, the murdering of Mormons and the massacring of Armenians, express much rather that aboriginal human neophobia, that pugnacity of which we all share the vestiges, and that inborn hatred of the alien and of eccentric and non-conforming men as aliens, than they express the positive piety of the various perpetrators. Piety is the mask, the inner force is tribal instinct.

14/15:5

James seems to have had a prescient vision of our headlines. It is estimated that there are some one hundred thousand Christian militants in this country. These are people who have distorted the non-violent message of Jesus and his compassionate outreach to the marginalized into a program of violence, prejudice, and hate. Our country today is these bigots' worst nightmare. A biracial President is reaching out a hand of fellowship and peace to Muslims. What outrage filled the air waves when the President in his speech in Cairo referred to the "holy" Qur'an. Doesn't he realize that only the Bible is a holy text?

As James so acutely observes, this really has nothing to do with true piety. He has correctly labeled this as "tribal instinct." One-narrative consciousness is a world of black and white, right and wrong, my way and the wrong way. It has one story for understanding the world. No one else's story has either relevance or significance. This "tribal instinct" can be found among Hindu, Jewish, Muslim, and Christian fanatics. This mindset constitutes the biggest enemy of true religion. The hate-filled fanatics it produces stand in sharp contrast to the God-centered models of religion we discussed in James's lectures on saintliness.

14/15:6 Unbalanced Devoutness

Let us take Devoutness. When unbalanced, one of its vices is called Fanaticism. Fanaticism (when not a mere expression of ecclesiastical ambition) is only loyalty carried to a convulsive extreme. When an intensely loyal and narrow mind is once grasped by the feeling that a certain superhuman person is worthy of its exclusive devotion, one of the first things that happens is that it idealizes the devotion itself. To adequately realize the merits of the idol gets to be considered the one great merit of the worshiper; and the sacrifices and servilities by which savage tribesmen have from time immemorial exhibited their faithfulness to chieftains are now outbid in favor of the deity. Vocabularies are exhausted and languages altered in the attempt to praise him enough; death is looked on as gain if it attract his grateful notice; and the personal attitude of being his devotee becomes what one might almost call a new and exalted kind of professional specialty within the tribe.

14/15:6

James offers us an insightful definition of fanaticism: "loyalty carried to a convulsive extreme." True religion and fanaticism relate like true patriotism and nationalism. I describe fanaticism as third-order fundamentalism. Three S's characterize fundamentalist thought, wherever it is found. It tends to be selective, simplistic, and static. It quotes part of the tradition but denies other parts. It interprets what it quotes in a literalist sense, without subtlety or nuance. And it freezes a living and growing tradition to a fictional point of certitude.

Fundamentalism comes in three varieties, three orders, or three levels of intensity. There is a first-order fundamentalism in which an enclave culture exists turned in upon itself with little interest in the outside world. An example of this is the way the Amish talk about "the English." In second-order fundamentalism, however, someone has challenged the enclave. A Jew becomes the high school principal in a little town where everyone is Methodist or Baptist. The enclave responds within the parameters of law, pressuring the school board to fire the outsider.

Third-order fundamentalism is the fanaticism of which James speaks so eloquently in this passage. It represents one of the greatest dangers threatening our planet today. It is described as "supramoral" because it recognizes neither the law of the land nor its own ethical code. Its causes are so pure that the end justifies the means. It can torture our nation's enemies, kill abortion doctors, blow up gay night clubs, shoot people at prayer, or perpetrate any other kind of crime in the name of a skewed and twisted interpretation of religion.

14/15:7 THE GREAT TORCH-BEARERS

[The] belief in the essential sacredness of every one expresses itself to-day in all sorts of humane customs and reformatory institutions, and in a growing aversion to the death penalty and to brutality in punishment. The saints, with their extravagance of human tenderness, are the great torch-bearers of this belief, the tip of the wedge, the clearers of the darkness. Like the single drops which sparkle in the sun as they are flung far ahead of the advancing edge of a wave-crest or of a flood, they show the way and are forerunners. The world is not yet with them, so they often seem in the midst of the world's affairs to be preposterous. Yet they are impregnators of the world, vivifiers and animaters of potentialities of goodness which but for them would lie forever dormant.

14/15:7

"The death penalty" and "brutality in punishment"! How could James be more relevant to our lives today? With an atavistic fervor, many Americans still cling to the idea that killing people somehow teaches them how much we value life. Orwellian vocabulary increases exponentially as we discuss "enhanced interrogation methods," including the water-boarding that was one of the crimes for which Nazis were held responsible in the Nuremberg trials.

Where can we turn? We can, of course, listen to the one-narrative voices. It's justifiable to torture "towel-heads" because they are not fully human. It's acceptable to execute criminals since most of them are poor and ignorant people of color, usually drug addicts, hardly human beings meriting either respect or justice. Or we can listen to the voices of higher consciousness. They are the "torch-bearers," showing us what heights we can reach when we evolve spiritually. To the inhabitants of one-narrative consciousness they appear as hopeless and deluded idealists. But for those who venture to come out of the basements of consciousness, they announce our only viable future, our only sustainable hope.

14/15:8 THE MORAL EQUIVALENT OF WAR

One hears of the mechanical equivalent of heat. What we now need to discover in the social realm is the moral equivalent of war: something heroic that will speak to men as universally as war does, and yet will be as compatible with their spiritual selves as war has proved itself to be incompatible.

14/15:8

James wrote an entire essay expanding the message encapsulated in these two sentences. Few things are as exciting as war, especially to one-narrative minds eager to create peace by eliminating all their enemies. What then would be a moral equivalent of war? Can the energy and imagination poured into peace-making and non-violent conflict resolution one day be seen as more exciting than the resources we now pour into our war machinery?

A friend of mine was at one point in his career the CEO of an advertising agency. He was approached by Tonka Toys for a contract to advertise some attack helicopters they were producing as children's toys. My friend persuaded them to produce rescue helicopters instead and the story merited coverage in the New York Times. This is just one small example of what can happen when we challenge ourselves to consider matters from a higher consciousness.

Jesus invited his listeners to preach from the housetops. He did not intend that they would literally crawl out onto their roofs, but that they would consistently try to speak from a higher consciousness. And this is James's challenge to his readers as well.

14/15:9 MORAL FITNESS

We have grown literally afraid to be poor. We despise any one who elects to be poor in order to simplify and save his inner life. If he does not join the general scramble and pant with the money-making street, we deem him spiritless and lacking in ambition. We have lost the power even of imagining what the ancient idealization of poverty could have meant: the liberation from material attachments, the unbribed soul, the manlier indifference, the paying our way by what we are or do and not by what we have, the right to fling away our life at any moment irresponsibly—the more athletic trim, in short, the moral fighting shape.

14/15:9

This is no easy sell in our consumer society. A nearby university has as its motto: "to live simply so that others may simply live." A Quaker meeting not far from me asks of its members a "testimony of simplicity." This means that a potential member should examine her lifestyle, trying to eliminate conspicuous consumption and empty displays of affluence. Economic crises and unemployment force many families to realize that some of the things they had thought were necessities were really luxuries.

I recently taught a three-week summer course called "The Way of the Monk." The students explored Hindu, Buddhist, and Christian monasticism. The third week of the course was spent on a seminary grounds where the students lived a quasi-monastic life: meditating three times a day, putting away their cell phones, maintaining silence during much of the day. This dramatically counter-cultural experience was deemed eminently worthwhile by the student participants. One of them wrote in his journal that it led him to challenge his tendency to judge people by the size of their houses or the value of their cars. I believe that James would have approved.

LECTURES XVI AND XVII
MYSTICISM

16/17:1 INEFFABILITY

The handiest of the marks by which I classify a state of mind as mystical is negative. The subject of it immediately says that it defies expression, that no adequate report of its contents can be given in words. It follows from this that its quality must be directly experienced; it cannot be imparted or transferred to others. In this peculiarity mystical states are more like states of feeling than like states of intellect. No one can make clear to another who has never had a certain feeling, in what the quality or worth of it consists. One must have musical ears to know the value of a symphony; one must have been in love one's self to understand a lover's state of mind.

16/17:1

We come now to what I consider to be the core of James's revolution. Having examined extensively the statements mystics make about their experiences, James is ready to organize this material in terms of four criteria. The first of these is ineffability. Because the mystical consciousness is essentially a unity consciousness, it necessarily transcends the duality of ordinary language. From childhood we were taught that if there is light there is dark, if there is up there is down, if there is cat, then there is non-cat. But this kind of barrier disappears in mystical consciousness. "*Tat tvam asi*," says the Hindu mystic: "You are that." You are one with what you are defining as other.

Because ordinary language, adequate for our dualistic world of experience, cannot stretch to this higher consciousness, the mystic must use the language of poetry. As Emily Dickenson has stated, the poet must tell the truth but tell it slant. One uses words to elicit an experience that transcends the literalness of the words used. The Vietnamese Buddhist teacher, Thich Nhat Hahn, urges us to develop new words: I-with-am; you-with-are etc. Language must be shaped in new ways and invested with new meaning. The mystics can give us little more than cryptic hints of the world of meaning they are inviting us to share.

16/17:2 NOETIC QUALITY

Although so similar to states of feeling, mystical states seem to those who experience them to be also states of knowledge. They are states of insight into depths of truth unplumbed by the discursive intellect. They are illuminations, revelations, full of significance and importance, all inarticulate though they remain; and as a rule they carry with them a curious sense of authority for after-time.

16/17:2

If ordinary language falls short of these experiences, then we might conclude that such experiences must be at a strictly emotional level, without knowledge content. For knowledge can only be known within the limits of reason. "No," responds the mystic. Their consistent claim is that what they know in their mystical experience is truer than anything known through reason. *Nous* is the Greek word for mind and *noetic* is its adjectival form. These mystics claim that their minds are active in these moments of illumination. There are things that they know more deeply and more surely than anything known through the processes of reason.

The 14th century mystic, Meister Eckhart, assures us many times in his writings that he is fully aware of God in his mystical experiences, and that this knowledge is more certain than anything he has attained through study or sense perception. Teresa of Avila, 16th century mystic and saint, claims that she was not able to learn much through books, but that she herself became a book written by God through her mystical experiences. These sentiments are repeated in all the traditions, at all times, and in all places. The mystics do not merely feel, they know.

16/17:3 TRANSIENCY

Mystical states cannot be sustained for long. Except in rare instances, half an hour, or at most an hour or two, seems to be the limit beyond which they fade into the light of common day. Often, when faded, their quality can but imperfectly be reproduced in memory; but when they recur it is recognized; and from one recurrence to another it is susceptible of continuous development in what is felt as inner richness and importance.

16/17:3

Mystics in various sacred traditions agree that these visitations are transient. Their departure is as mysterious as their arrival. And yet, although they disappear, they are not entirely gone. Hindus point to the analogy of plunging their robes into the dye that gives them their deep ocher color. The robes can absorb only so much color through one immersion in the dye. So they are hung out to dry and then immersed again. The second time creates a richer color and the third time even more so.

As the human consciousness is plunged into the vat of mystic color, only so much can be absorbed. But when it is submerged again, the color darkens. Finally one comes to an almost constant state of mystic awareness, a consciousness that lives most comfortably on that roof deck of our house of consciousness, a place most souls reach only on rare occasions, if at all.

16/17:4 PASSIVITY

Although the oncoming of mystical states may be facilitated by preliminary voluntary operations, as by fixing the attention, or going through certain bodily performances, or in other ways which manuals of mysticism prescribe; yet when the characteristic sort of consciousness once has set in, the mystic feels as if his own will were in abeyance, and indeed sometimes as if he were grasped and held by a superior power.

16/17:4

Passivity feels somehow negative. Describing someone as a "passive person" hardly seems a compliment. But James speaks here of something more profound, something reminiscent of grace and gift. We can prepare ourselves for such experiences by various spiritual exercises: silence, chanting, fasting, walks in nature, and meditation. But we cannot make them happen. There is no celestial gumball machine into which we can insert our quarter and expect by right to receive a mystical experience.

This touches on the whole dynamic of grace and good works that fills so many libraries. It is a both-and reality, not an either-or dichotomy. It resembles the process by which two people become friends. No one can make you their friend. You would resent being asked the price of your friendship. On the other hand, people certainly can say and do things that make it more likely for you to offer them your friendship. It is much the same in our relations to that infinite mystery from which mystical experiences arise.

16/17:5 ERSATZ ECSTASY

The sway of alcohol over mankind is unquestionably due to its power to stimulate the mystical faculties of human nature, usually crushed to earth by the cold facts and dry criticisms of the sober hour. Sobriety diminishes, discriminates, and says no; drunkenness expands, unites, and says yes. It is in fact the great exciter of the *Yes* function in man. It brings its votary from the chill periphery of things to the radiant core. It makes him for the moment one with truth. Not through mere perversity do men run after it. To the poor and the unlettered it stands in the place of symphony concerts and of literature; and it is part of the deeper mystery and tragedy of life that whiffs and gleams of something that we immediately recognize as excellent should be vouchsafed to so many of us only in the fleeting earlier phases of what in its totality is so degrading a poisoning.

16/17:5

James offers us in this passage an extraordinary insight into the role of intoxicants in various cultures. Human beings desire higher consciousness. But when they don't know how to find it in legitimate ways, they will seek it in ways often harmful to their health. On the other hand, when people discover the "natural high" of meditation or sacred dance, of sports or hiking in the mountains, of deep friendships and exciting learning opportunities, they tend to experience no strong temptation to use harmful drugs.

As dean of students, I saw that "Just Say No" programs inevitably failed. Through reading James, I tried another approach by inviting some of our trustees to fund a coffeehouse on campus. This proved to be an extremely attractive option for students. It was a good place to study or just "hang out" and there was even a small stage for poetry readings and music. Students didn't come there to say "no" to alcohol; they came there to say "yes" to a good time; and it just happened that the good time did not include alcohol.

16/17:6 One Point on the Spectrum

[O]ur normal waking consciousness, rational consciousness as we call it, is but one special type of consciousness, whilst all about it, parted from it by the filmiest of screens, there lie potential forms of consciousness entirely different. We may go through life without suspecting their existence; but apply the requisite stimulus, and at a touch they are there in all their completeness, definite types of mentality which probably somewhere have their field of application and adaptation. No account of the universe in its totality can be final which leaves these other forms of consciousness quite disregarded.

16/17:6

The first sentence of this passage has proved to be the most frequently quoted sentence in his book. It articulates the very core of James's revolution. Imagine yourself believing that your TV had only one channel and then discovering one day that you had access to hundreds more. Human beings are capable of alternate states of consciousness. Failure to recognize this results in living a depleted life. A good deal of the unhappiness and depression experienced by so many Americans, despite our affluence, may well be traceable to a failure to appreciate the truth of what James has so clearly stated in this passage.

The great scholar of world religions, Huston Smith, described taking a group of American students to visit a noted Hindu teacher in India. He asked the teacher what difference there was between American education and the kind of education taking place in a Hindu ashram. The teacher responded that, whereas American education took place at only one level of consciousness (what James calls "normal waking consciousness"), ashram education was at four levels: waking consciousness, dream consciousness, non-dream sleep consciousness, and mystical consciousness.

16/17:7 REACHING UNANIMITY

This overcoming of all the usual barriers between the individual and the Absolute is the great mystic achievement. In mystic states we both become one with the Absolute and we become aware of our oneness. This is the everlasting and triumphant mystical tradition, hardly altered by differences of clime or creed. In Hinduism, in Neoplatonism, in Sufism, in Christian mysticism, in Whitmanism, we find the same recurring note, so that there is about mystical utterances an eternal unanimity which ought to make a critic stop and think, and which brings it about that the mystical classics have, as has been said, neither birthday nor native land.

16/17:7

Within this spectrum, the highest consciousness is mystical consciousness. We find this recognized in virtually all of the sacred traditions. The chief characteristic of this consciousness is the transcendence of all dualism. It is, in other words, a unity consciousness. Imagine yourself looking at an ocean and noticing the many waves. You might count them or even name them. Now imagine yourself shifting your focus from the plurality of waves to the oneness of water. Analogously, most of us focus on the discrete identity of the many things surrounding us: persons, animals, plants, and diverse objects. The mystic, however, has as the focus of awareness the one divine mystery manifested in each of these forms. Where we see many, the mystics see one.

One might think of the visual exercises we often find in psychology textbooks. If we look at the picture one way, we see a vase; but if we can shift our perspective, we see the profile of two people facing each other. For a mystic, the focus has shifted. The higher order, the transcendent mystery, is seen in all its myriad manifestations. The duality between "this" and "that" disappears; the field of vision is unified, a vision unutterably beautiful, mysteriously one. The diverse descriptions of this transformation of consciousness are remarkably similar, despite all differences in religion, nationality, and language.

16/17:8 CHARACTERISTICS OF MYSTICAL STATES

My next task is to inquire whether we can invoke it as authoritative. Does it furnish any warrant for the truth of the twice-bornness and supernaturality and pantheism which it favors?

1. Mystical states, when well developed, usually are, and have the right to be, absolutely authoritative over the individuals to whom they come.
2. No authority emanates from them which should make it a duty for those who stand outside of them to accept their revelations uncritically.
3. They break down the authority of the non-mystical or rationalistic consciousness, based upon the understanding and the senses alone. They show it to be only one kind of consciousness. They open out the possibility of other orders of truth, in which, so far as anything in us vitally responds to them, we may freely continue to have faith.

16/17:8

Of what use are mystical experiences to those of us who inhabit less exalted states of consciousness? Whatever the mystics know at this level has authority only for them. And yet, if all the sacred traditions point to exemplars of this kind of consciousness and if the people who embody this consciousness share a common profile of wisdom, compassion, humility, peace of mind, and an abiding joy, then might there not be a message here for all of us?

One might argue that all that these mystics have in common is some form of delusion. And yet, there appears to be a clear line of demarcation between the people we institutionalize as delusional and the extraordinarily healthy and productive personalities identified as mystics. Even if we have had no mystical experiences of our own, it seems reasonable to at least entertain the possibility that there is something going on here that is very real, something entirely within the capacity of our human nature. If I see concert musicians in rapture as they play, even if I personally possess a minimum of musical appreciation, I would surely be reasonable in concluding that what these musicians experience is legitimate and real, a higher development of something I can appreciate only at a lower level of personal experience.

16/17:9 TRUEST OF INSIGHTS

Mystical states indeed wield no authority due simply to their being mystical states. But the higher ones among them point in directions to which the religious sentiments even of non-mystical men incline. They tell of the supremacy of the ideal, of vastness, of union, of safety, and of rest. They offer us *hypotheses*, hypotheses which we may voluntarily ignore, but which as thinkers we cannot possibly upset. The super-naturalism and optimism to which they would persuade us may, interpreted in one way or another, be after all the truest of insights into the meaning of this life.

16/17:9

James invites us to think about the role hypotheses play in our learning process. Hypotheses are not proven facts. They are working premises prompting further verification. Perhaps my hypothesis in the 1950s was that human beings would someday be able to walk on the surface of the moon. When I sat in front of my television screen in 1969 and watched a human being walking on the moon, my hypothesis had become a proven fact.

Many of my first year students approach their first day of college with more optimism because they have siblings who are college graduates. If their brothers or sisters survived and earned undergraduate degrees, then they could surely do the same. Perhaps the mystics are humankind's older brothers and sisters. They go before us, modeling a consciousness that we can someday experience as our own. They are the pioneers of the human potential for consciousness transformation.

LECTURE XVIII
PHILOSOPHY

18:1 Unwholesome Privacy

Feeling is private and dumb, and unable to give an account of itself. It allows that its results are mysteries and enigmas, declines to justify them rationally, and on occasion is willing that they should even pass for paradoxical and absurd. Philosophy takes just the opposite attitude. Her aspiration is to reclaim from mystery and paradox whatever territory she touches. To find an escape from obscure and wayward personal persuasion to truth objectively valid for all thinking men has ever been the intellect's most cherished ideal. To redeem religion from unwholesome privacy, and to give public status and universal right of way to its deliverances, has been reason's task.

18:1

We meet in this passage the paradox of studying religious experience. Most disciplines offer reasonable interpretations of activities that can themselves be understood by reason. One can, for example, make a reasonable argument for preferring a democratic form of government to a socialist state. But the study of religious experience doesn't fit this model. The testimonies of the mystics claim to transcend reason. It seems that we have no choice but to abandon any effort to deal with them rationally, relegating them to the arena of mere opinion or personal taste. And as we have all been taught: "*De gustibus nil disputandum*"—there can be no rational argument about matters of taste. It is simply not possible to craft a reasonable argument to convince you to enjoy sushi if you are repelled by the idea of eating raw fish.

James argues, however, that although the content of these experiences claims to be beyond the reach of reason, there is nothing hindering us from employing a reasonable methodology in the study of what claims to be trans-rational data. We can, for example, explore what these experiences have in common. We can objectively study the characteristics of the people claiming to have these experiences. This was James's goal: "to redeem religion from unwholesome privacy." I would argue that, within the limits of the data available to him, he achieved that goal and thus launched the systematic study of religious experience that continues to this day.

18:2 Presumptuous Intellectualism

The intellectualism in religion which I wish to discredit pretends to be something altogether different from this. It assumes to construct religious objects out of the resources of logical reason alone, or of logical reason drawing rigorous inference from non-subjective facts. It calls its conclusions dogmatic theology, or philosophy of the absolute, as the case may be; it does not call them science of religions. It reaches them in an *a priori* way, and warrants their veracity.

18:2

The content of James's study falls in the realm of the purportedly trans-rational. But the methodology he employs in his investigations is rational. He contrasts his "science of religion" with philosophies or theologies claiming that their conclusions are *a priori* true. One thinks, for example, of an argument common to fundamentalist Christians that the Bible should be understood as God's Word because there are passages in the Bible making this claim. Most reasonable people would judge this to be a circular and therefore invalid argument. James would concur.

James regards this kind of thinking as an unwarranted kind of "intellectualism." His own study proceeds with greater caution. He examines the experiences on which religions are ultimately based. He looks at them through a comparative lens, seeing where they are similar or dissimilar. He lists the fruits of these religions, as well as the figures judged to be their exemplars. He distinguishes results that follow from co-opted forms of religion from results that follow from the religion itself. In our day, for example, we distinguish the acts of religious terrorists in their distortion of their sacred traditions from the acts of those who truly follow their religion's authentic teachings.

LECTURE XIX
OTHER CHARACTERISTICS

19:1 SACRIFICE

In most books on religion, three things are represented as its most essential elements. These are Sacrifice, Confession, and Prayer.... First of Sacrifice. Sacrifices to gods are omnipresent in primeval worship; but, as cults have grown refined, burnt offerings and the blood of he-goats have been superseded by sacrifices more spiritual in their nature. Judaism, Islam, and Buddhism get along without ritual sacrifice; so does Christianity, save in so far as the notion is preserved in transfigured form in the mystery of Christ's atonement. These religions substitute offerings of the heart, renunciations of the inner self, for all those vain oblations.

19:1

James turns now to "other characteristics" of religion. Sacrifice is a common religious practice. But in studying the history of religion, we see how the understanding of sacrifice reflects the community's level of consciousness. At a tribal level, animal sacrifice is common. But at a more evolved level, the understanding of sacrifice changes.

Consider Judaism. Animal sacrifice prevails throughout biblical history, from Cain's and Abel's sacrifices to the burnt offerings of Temple sacrifice in the 60s of the first century of the Common Era. But with the Roman destruction of the Second Temple, the rabbis taught that the times of prayer in the synagogue replaced the sacrifices formerly offered in the Temple. After all, it was the worship of the heart that was symbolized in the sacrificed animals, and that worship could now be best expressed in the prayers of the community.

19:2 RELIGION IN ACT

Prayer is religion in act; that is, prayer is real religion. It is prayer that distinguishes the religious phenomenon from such similar or neighboring phenomena as purely moral or aesthetic sentiment. Religion is nothing if it be not the vital act by which the entire mind seeks to save itself by clinging to the principle from which it draws its life. This act is prayer...the very movement itself of the soul, putting itself in a personal relation of contact with the mysterious power of which it feels the presence.... Wherever this interior prayer is lacking, there is no religion; wherever, on the other hand, this prayer rises and stirs the soul, even in the absence of forms or of doctrines, we have living religion.

19:2

James points to prayer as "real religion." The Jewish philosopher and religious thinker, Martin Buber, once remarked that all levels of creations aspire to what lies above them. Thus plants at their highest level become carnivores, capable of ingesting insects and small pieces of meat. And animals, as every owner of a pet can testify, seem at times to be stretching to communicate with their masters in human language. What then about people? What are we humans when we are standing, so to speak, on tiptoes? Buber asserts that this happens when we are praying.

There is another story about Buber on this topic. Someone told him that Sigmund Freud had asserted that a full human life consisted of success in love and work, i.e., intimate relationships and fulfilling activity. *Lieben* und *arbeiten* were Freud's actual words. We're told that when Buber heard this teaching of Freud, he stroked his beard and said: "*Lieben und arbeiten, lieben und arbeiten, ja, doch auch beten.*" "Loving and working, loving and working, yes, but also praying." For Buber, unlike the atheist Freud, there could be no full development of our human potential without prayer.

19:3 THE WIDE-OPEN DOOR

[I]n religion we have a department of human nature with unusually close relations to the transmarginal or subliminal region. If the word "subliminal" is offensive to any of you…call it by any other name you please, to distinguish it from the level of full sunlit consciousness. Call this latter the A-region of personality, if you care to, and call the other the B-region. The B-region, then, is obviously the larger part of each of us, for it is the abode of everything that is latent and the reservoir of everything that passes unrecorded or unobserved…. In persons deep in the religious life…the door into this region seems unusually wide open.

19:3

Our conscious mind is but the tip of an iceberg. There are various names we give to what lies below: the trans-marginal (what is somehow outside the box), the subliminal (literally what slips in under the threshold), the unconscious, the subconscious, the B-region. Call it what we will, there is abundant testimony to its existence. A characteristic common to mystics is their ability to somehow connect with this territory that lies beyond the maps of the majority of human beings. They have an ability to pick up messages from a larger field of awareness than most people access.

I spoke once to an old Jesuit who had been a bishop in India for many years. He told me that he frequently visited a Hindu holy man in his area, someone for whom the bishop had a deep respect. As they were conversing one day, the holy man doubled over, convulsed in pain. The bishop heard him say, "All those poor people. All those poor people." The bishop happened to glance at his watch and noticed the time of day: 2:15pm. Returning to his house, the bishop turned on the radio. The ordinary programming was interrupted for a news item. A train had crashed some hundred miles away from where the bishop and the holy man had been speaking, and over two hundred people were killed. The time of the crash was 2:15pm.

LECTURE XX
CONCLUSIONS

20:1 A Broad Summary

Summing up in the broadest possible way the characteristics of the religious life, as we have found them, it includes the following beliefs:—

1. That the visible world is part of a more spiritual universe from which it draws its chief significance;
2. That union or harmonious relation with that higher universe is our true end;
3. That prayer or inner communion with the spirit thereof—be that spirit "God" or "law"—is a process wherein work is really done, and spiritual energy flows in and produces effects, psychological or material, within the phenomenal world.

20:1

Summarizing his investigation, James finds three insights shared by the mystics. First, what we immediately experience resides within a larger frame of reference. This may be called God or the Tao, Satchitananda or Wakan Tonka; but the core idea is the same.

Second, our goals as humans cannot be met within the smaller framework. Our most abundant life can only be found by our alignment with that larger order. One recalls the words of the great mystic, Augustine of Hippo: "*Inquietum est cor nostrum, Domine, donec quiescat in Te.*" "Our heart is restless, O Lord, until it rests in You." And then there is the assertion of one of the great masters of psychology, Carl Gustav Jung, that he had never successfully dealt with a client over thirty years of age without exploring the region of their spiritual life, their connection with the larger reality of the Spirit.

Third, prayer is a real action in the world. It has effects. We are not limited by our physical activities. As a colleague of mine likes to say, when you change your mind about something in the privacy of your home, the whole universe is somehow changed. This assertion is beginning to make more sense now that we live in a post-Heisenberg world, a world in which so-called objective matter is somehow affected by the intentions of the scientists working with it.

20:2 Psychological Characteristics

Religion includes also the following psychological characteristics:—

4. A new zest which adds itself like a gift to life, and takes the form either of lyrical enchantment or of appeal to earnestness and heroism.
5. An assurance of safety and a temper of peace, and, in relation to others, a preponderance of loving affections.

20:2

James refers here to the profile of the mystic formed by comparing the evidences of the various traditions when describing their heroes of faith, the highest exemplars of their respective religions. Great energy surges through the mystics. No longer compelled to defend themselves against the "slings and arrows of outrageous Fortune," they are free to live heroically in our midst. The energy so many people divert to the support of their neuroses is freed up to be channeled into the overarching unity of life as it is lived by saints and mystics.

Great peace of soul and compassion are the most evident fruits of living at this level of consciousness. Asked in a recent interview whether he ever experienced the loss of peace of soul, the Dalai Lama smiled gently and said "no." He admitted to a level of minor frustrations, but not to anything able to dislodge his constant abiding in a deeply experienced peace and joy. And flowing from this peace is the evident compassion he displays in all his encounters with others. This pattern is found across the board in all the practitioners of religion who reach a similar level of attainment.

Lecture XX

20:3 Partial Systems

We must frankly recognize the fact that we live in partial systems, and that parts are not interchangeable in the spiritual life. If we are peevish and jealous, destruction of the self must be an element of our religion; why need it be one if we are good and sympathetic from the outset? If we are sick souls, we require a religion of deliverance; but why think so much of deliverance, if we are healthy-minded? Unquestionably, some men have the completer experience and the higher vocation, here just as in the social world; but for each man to stay in his own experience, whate'er it be, and for others to tolerate him there, is surely best.

20:3

James moves towards the end of his investigation with conciliatory words. He shows a truth that is central to all authentic spiritual growth and practice. It is best "for each man to stay in his own experience" and "for others to tolerate him there." Buddhist wisdom admonishes us not to try to do another person's practice. There are a number of circumstances leading us to our present state of mind, to the consciousness we most regularly inhabit. James eschews all proselytizing and violent efforts to change others.

Change and growth come best by gentle invitation. Seeing people with greater social skills might motivate us to develop in that regard. Being connected with the great saints and mystics might lead us to try to act in that larger universe of awareness that they so comfortably inhabit. But we shouldn't push ourselves nor should we be pushed by others. Buddhism tells us that when the student is ready, the teacher will appear. James might well be the teacher that some of us were waiting for. But if not, then put James aside. What is unattractive today may well be attractive tomorrow.

20:4 A DISTANT GOD

The God whom science recognizes must be a God of universal laws exclusively, a God who does a wholesale, not a retail business. He cannot accommodate his processes to the convenience of individuals. The bubbles on the foam which coats a stormy sea are floating episodes, made and unmade by the forces of the wind and water. Our private selves are like those bubbles…their destinies weigh nothing and determine nothing in the world's irremediable currents of events.

20:4

The God deduced in Aristotle's Metaphysics is neither a God capable of loving us nor a God we would be motivated to love. Aristotle's God is little more than an entity required by reason to get the universe functioning, much like the electricity enabling this computer and the lights in my office to operate. The God of the rationalist philosophers is a God who lives within systems of reason. Sometimes philosophers attempt to prove this God, while other thinkers strive with equal energy to dismantle those proofs.

These debates mean little to people who inhabit the realm of religious experience. Thomas Aquinas put down his pen, leaving unfinished his great summation of theology. He told his secretary, Reginald of Piperno, that his mystical experiences had become so intense that the arguments of reason "seemed like straw." Reason is useful up to a point, but for those who move into trans-rational realms, reason is a guide unable to do more than bring us to the border.

20:5 THE "MORE"

Let me then propose, as an hypothesis, that whatever it may be on its *farther* side, the "more" with which in religious experience we feel ourselves connected is on its *hither* side the subconscious continuation of our conscious life.

20:5

Again a hypothesis. Not a certain truth but something to be tested in the crucible of our experience. There is clearly a subconscious realm, that much is a psychological fact. Mystics claim that this realm is itself a face of God. Just as the divine suffuses the external world of nature, so, too, does that same divine reality live and move in the realm of the subconscious. James can neither prove nor disprove this divine reality. He does not claim to be a mystic himself, only a humble student of mysticism. What James does assert, however, is that the greater realm with which religion asserts a connection, if it truly exists, is on the human side connected with what he calls "the subconscious continuation of our conscious life."

It is an adage of religion that one cannot deeply know oneself without knowing the divine mystery and conversely one cannot deeply know the divine mystery without knowing oneself. For Jung, the same archetype refers both to the divine and to the individuated self. Our deepest reality lies in being God-centered. Holiness in the last analysis is wholeness.

20:6 GOD WINS

This world may indeed, as science assures us, some day burn up or freeze; but if it is part of his order, the old ideals are sure to be brought elsewhere to fruition, so that where God is, tragedy is only provisional and partial, and shipwreck and dissolution are not the absolutely final things.

20:6

How does it all end, with a whimper or with a bang? For a mystic like Paul, the final end of everything is when God will be all in all. Or, as a Jewish mystic expresses this truth: God rolls up the universe like a Torah scroll and puts it back in the ark of eternity. The common faith of those who share deep religious experience is that God does indeed win in the end. And God's win is not our loss. Quite to the contrary, we very much win as well, a greater win than we could possibly imagine within the limited horizons of our thought.

The German mystical tradition assures us that "*Ein begriffener Gott ist kein Gott*"—"A God we can conceptualize or understand is not God at all." Or as the ancient Tao Te Ching reminds us in its opening words: "The Tao that can be named is not the eternal Tao." Whatever fits within the limits of our minds and language can never be the Limitless, the Nameless, the Eternal. Where rational investigation stops, only a personal experience of what lies beyond can suffice.

SELECT BIBLIOGRAPHY

BOOKS BY WILLIAM JAMES:

The Principles of Psychology, 2 vols. (1890). Dover Publications: New York, 1950.

The Will to Believe and Other Essays in Popular Philosophy (1897). Cosimo, Inc: New York, 2006.

The Varieties of Religious Experience: A Study in Human Nature. Longmans Green: New York, 1902.

Pragmatism: A New Name for Some Old Ways of Thinking (1907). Dover Publications: New York, 1995.

A Pluralistic Universe (1909). University of Nebraska Press, 1996.

The Meaning of Truth: A Sequel to "Pragmatism" (1909). Prometheus Books: New York, 1997.

Some Problems of Philosophy: A Beginning of an Introduction to Philosophy (1911). University of Nebraska Press, 1996.

BOOKS ABOUT WILLIAM JAMES:

Barzun, Jacques. *Stroll with William James.* Harper & Row Publishers: New York, 1983.

Bird, Graham. *William James.* Routledge & Kegan Paul: New York, 1986.

Cotkin, George. *William James, Public Philosopher.* The John Hopkins University Press: Baltimore, 1990.

Fisher, Paul. *House of Wits: An Intimate Portrait of the James Family.* Henry Holt and Company: New York, 2008.

Lewis, R.W.B. *The Jameses: A Family Narrative.* Farrar, Straus and Giroux: New York, 1991.

Myers, Gerald E. *William James: His Life and Thought.* Yale University Press: New Haven, 1986.

Perry, Ralph B. *The Thought and Character of William James. 2 vols.* Little, Brown, and Company: Boston, 1935.

Ramsey, Bennett. *Submitting to Freedom: The Religious Vision of William James.* Oxford University Press: New York, 1993.

Suckiel, Ellen Kappy. *Heaven's Champion: William James's Philosophy of Religion.* University of Notre Dame Press: Indiana, 1996.

ARTICLES ABOUT WILLIAM JAMES:

Anderson, Doug. "Respectability and the Wild Beasts of the Philosophical Desert: The Heart of James's Varieties." *The Journal of Speculative Philosophy* Vol. 17, No. 1, 2003.

Christenson, Tom, and Kurt Keljo. "On the Relation of Morality and Religion: Two Lessons from James's 'Varieties of Religious Experience.'" *Journal of Moral Education,* 2003.

Madsen, Catherine. "What James Knew." *Cross Currents* Vol. 53, No 3, 2003.

Slater, Michael. "Metaphysical Intimacy and the Moral Life: The Ethical Project of 'The Varieties of Religious Experience.'" *Transactions of the Charles Peirce Society* Vol. 43 No. 1, 2007.

To order additional copies of
William James's Revolution, please visit

www.ronmillersworld.org